SHARK TALES

TRUE (AND AMAZING) STORIES FROM AMERICA'S LAWYERS

Ron Liebman

A TOUCHSTONE BOOK
PUBLISHED BY SIMON & SCHUSTER
NEW YORK LONDON TORONTO SYDNEY SINGAPORE

 TOUCHSTONE
Rockefeller Center
1230 Avenue of the Americas
New York, NY 10020

First Touchstone Edition 2001

TOUCHSTONE and colophon are registered trademarks of
Simon & Schuster, Inc.

Designed by Kyoko Watanabe

Manufactured in the United States of America

10 9 8 7 6 5 4 3 2

The Library of Congress has cataloged the Simon & Schuster edition as follows:
    Shark tales : true (and amazing) stories from America's lawyers / [compiled by]
Ron Liebman
        p. cm.
    1. Law—United States—Anecdotes.   2. Law—United States—Humor.
    3. Practice of law—United States.   4. Justice, Administration of—United States.
    I. Liebman, Ronald S.
    K184.S535 2000
    349.73'02'07—dc21   00-030786

ISBN 0-684-85728-6
      0-7432-0371-2 (Pbk)

Contents

PART V

SHARK TALES

(shark) n. 1. Any of various predatory fishes with a rough, scaleless skin. 2. A person who preys greedily on others. 2. Informal. One with unusual ability in a particular field.

Random House Webster's Concise Dictionary

For a good time, hire a hooker.
For a lot of time, hire my lawyer.

Anonymous Prison Cell Graffito

Introduction

THREE FRIENDS—A DOCTOR, A PRIEST, AND A LAWYER—ARE fishing in a boat out in the ocean. From out of nowhere a huge gust of wind slams into them, capsizes the boat, and hurls them overboard. Gasping for breath, spitting seawater, they desperately hang on to the boat's hull. Things get worse: a school of ferocious sharks swims toward the capsized boat and immediately starts circling, closing in for the kill.

Terrified, the priest closes his eyes, raises his face to heaven, and begins praying. The doctor is imagining who will die first.

Then, without a word, the lawyer pushes off from the capsized boat and swims for shore. The sharks immediately open their circle and let him pass.

The priest opens his eyes, sees what has just happened, and with the joy of the truly devout, exclaims, "It's a miracle! A miracle!"

"Miracle, hell," responds the doctor. "That, my friend, is professional courtesy."

Beginning, I suppose with Shakespeare's famous line about killing all the lawyers, right through to the miles and miles of lawyer jokes that litter the landscape of modern times, the public has had a fascination—and weird attitude—toward lawyers. Lawyers seem to be held simultaneously in low esteem and high regard. Lawyers may be the butt of joke upon joke, but what is the first thing we do when we've been aggrieved, when someone or something has taken unfair advantage of us? Or more to the point, harmed us? That's right, we reach for a lawyer.

And how we love stories about lawyers; can't seem to satisfy our taste for them. Lawyer novels, lawyer movies. They have become permanent residents in our top-ten lists.

And we lawyers. We are a mixed lot. In America we are about as diverse as the population that comprises our clients. We love the lawyer jokes as much as you do. But you know what? There's another side to the jokes and stories. An inside side, if you will.

We lawyers see so many different people and situations during the course of our work. The experiences we accumulate while representing our clients literally run the gamut of the human condition. Put a bunch of lawyers together in a relaxed atmosphere, and sooner or later we start swapping stories of our experiences. Not the stuff that's confidential and privileged, but the truly funny, interesting, and on occasion heartfelt things that happen in court, or in witness interviews, or while we're otherwise preparing and presenting our cases.

I've got stories. Most lawyers do. I thought it might be fun to collect some of them and share them with a wider audience than just us lawyers.

I began by soliciting stories, based on personal experiences, from lawyers around the country. My methodology was primitive. I wrote to lawyers and law firms mostly at random, my only self-imposed requirement to try to cover the four corners of our country. I asked for "your best story, the one you love to tell over and over." The response was wonderful. Of course, I asked some lawyer friends to share a good tale or two. And there are a few stories from our cousins at the bar in the United Kingdom. Our legal tradition and indeed our very legal system is directly descended from that of the Brits. Their experiences mirror our own, even if the mirror is somewhat distorted by powdered wigs and princely accents.

I also discovered a wonderful little book entitled *Disorder in the Court,* published by the National Court Reporters Association. The nation's court reporters and stenographers have heard it all. They have recorded verbatim every question and answer given at trial, or in depositions (those question-and-answer sessions lawyers have with witnesses pretrial in their law offices), every colloquy between counsel and the court. Preserved in the millions of pages of transcripts of legal proceedings are some of the funniest, most outrageous utterings imaginable. The NCRA collected and published some of the funniest. They have very kindly permitted me to reprint a selection of some of them here. I remain grateful to them. I also commend their full collection to you. The National Court Reporters Association can be reached at 8224 Old Courthouse Road, Vienna, VA 22182.

Join us, your lawyers, as we swap stories, all experienced while working for you.

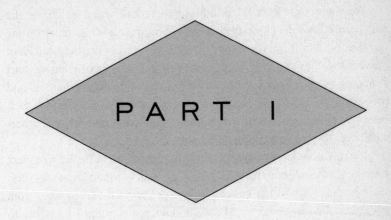

PART I

SEX, SEX, AND MORE SEX

THERE WAS THIS GUY IN MY LAW SCHOOL CLASS. ALTHOUGH I can't remember his name (I think it was Bob something or other), I can still picture the two of us walking down the street near the law school one autumn day during lunch break. This was the late sixties, so I suppose we were wearing bell-bottoms and sixties hair. I do remember that Bob sported a handlebar mustache. Anyway, Bob was complaining. Not about the rigors of law school: the endless days of classes, the mountains of cases and statutes to read, the never-ending demands of our professors. No, Bob was focused on none of that. Bob was complaining about sex. To be precise, he was complaining about having too much sex. He was tired. Really tired. I'll explain.

Bob had a roommate. She was a nurse at the hospital affiliated with our university. I remember her, too. I had recently spent an evening at Bob's apartment listening to the new Beatles album that had been released earlier that day. It was the *White Album,* I can remember that vividly, can picture the three of us sitting on Bob's ratty furniture listening to the Beatles' new songs. Bob's roommate was still wearing her nurse's whites. She must have just arrived from work. She was pretty and blond, with a truly memorable figure that did wonderful things for that nurse's uniform.

Anyway, Bob and I were walking down the street, probably headed back to the law school after lunch, and he was complaining. Now, Bob was a complainer. He was from Minnesota and he complained about how cold the winters there were. But he also complained about how hot the summers were in the East where we were in school. Sometimes he complained about our professors. Law school is tough and most of us griped about things. But that day Bob's complaints about sex were not only truly heartfelt, there was also an important point to his predicament. I thought then, and believe now, thirty years later, that Bob was on to something.

So here we are walking back to class and Bob is complaining. It seems all his roommate wants to do is have sex. Bob's tired. He tells me that he came home from class the other night and once again there she was, lounging around the apartment in her underwear, letting him know she was ready. And she was hot. Shaking his head, as if to say, "Can you believe what I have to put up with?" he describes for me the bikini panties she was wearing, the lace peekaboo bra. Living in law student celibacy (I had moved back into my parents' home after college so as to better afford law school), my life consisted of study, the practice of some rudimentary hygiene, and listening to my mother fret about my eating habits and my father's warnings that the market was becoming glutted with lawyers.

Could I believe it? I could almost see it. Bob shakes his head. He tells me he has no energy left. Sex, sex, sex. That's all she wants from me, he tells me. Sex in the mornings, sex after class. Sex at night when he's trying to study. He's out of energy. He simply can't hold up. He's telling this to me, who hasn't had a date in weeks. I'm walking down the street with Bob, and listening to him, I feel like I might faint. But Bob goes on, shaking his head, describing his predicament in the kind of detail we lawyers-to-be were being trained to master.

And then Bob makes his point.

If there is one prime stimulant in life, he says, one thing that propels mankind forward, those who live in civilized society, and those who still live in the dark ages of primitive existence, it's sex. Walking back toward class, dragging his satiated bell-bottomed body toward the punishing burdens of academia, Bob understands. The law is nothing more than an intellectual harness, an ethereal straitjacket. All it does is constrain as best as possible human actions, the ins and outs of everyday life, virtually all of which are motivated by nothing more than the urge to have sex. In just about every action—in commerce, in our personal relationships with friends and neighbors, in just about all we do, Bob understands—sex is the prime motivator. It's the incessant itch, and the eternal need to scratch it, that drives human behavior. The law does nothing more than put a bandage over the spot so we don't scratch it sore.

"Man," Bob says, "if I could only find some way to harness that energy. Hell, I'd be the richest person in the world. I'd have the key to all human behavior. I'd understand every lawsuit, I'd have the key to winning every case."

Then he gets this sad little smile on his face, somberly shakes his head, almost whispers, "And I wouldn't have to . . ." Even today I can't repeat the way he described his sincere and earnest desire to find a way to perform less you-know-what with you-know-whom in her white, too-tight nurse's uniform. At the time, while listening to Bob's lament, I was eyeing a small spot in the middle of the street near where we were walking, thinking maybe I'd just lie down right there and wait patiently for the next transit bus to roll over me and put me out of my misery.

But, of course, Bob was on to something. Sex, the proverbial gas in our tanks, is pretty combustible stuff, propelling us at breakneck speed toward life's predicaments. And when the inevitable collision occurs, we lawyers are there at the scene.

The first group of tales I've assembled shares the common theme of what sex can get us into.

Hell Hath No Fury

I HAD COME INTO THE CASE AT THE BITTER END. OTHER DIVORCE lawyers had preceded me, all resigning because of the behavior of the parties.

My client was the husband, Mr. Jones (I've changed his name—you'll see why presently). Mr. Jones was the senior partner in one of Wall Street's most prestigious and prominent law firms. He had it all—a great position, wealth, a society wife, three perfect children, you name it. Mrs. Jones, perhaps a bit bored with the marriage, had suggested a trial separation. It was then that Mr. Jones became involved with another woman. When his girlfriend moved in with him, Mrs. Jones filed for divorce and launched a campaign to humiliate her husband and wipe him out financially.

During the years the case had been pending, Mr. Jones repeatedly tried to appease his wife. By the time I was retained, he had already turned over to her just about everything he owned. An important judgeship was awaiting him, so he was desperate to get the divorce done and over with. Adverse publicity, linking him to a messy divorce over a mistress, might have blocked his appointment. But Mrs. Jones was not to be satisfied.

On the day I'll never forget, Mr. Jones had virtually no assets left. She had gotten them all. The end was in sight. A meeting had been arranged. Mrs. Jones had agreed to final terms of divorce. At least that was what her lawyers had told me.

Mr. Jones and I entered the ornate wood-paneled conference room of Mrs. Jones's attorneys' law offices. Moments later we were joined by Mrs. Jones and her lawyer. Greetings were formal and cold. No hands were shaken. After we were seated, pens at the ready, a secretary entered and placed settlement papers in front of the parties. Finally, I remember thinking. Finally, this acrimonious case will come to an end.

Now, among their considerable formerly joint property, Mr. and Mrs.

Jones had possessed four automobiles. Mr. Jones had already delivered title to three of them—all luxury vehicles—to Mrs. Jones, as had been agreed. Mr. Jones had kept an old Volkswagen, its book value less than $1,000.

As I said, pens were out, we were ready to sign. That's when Mrs. Jones said, "I need the Volkswagen, too."

Mr. Jones looked at his wife with clear astonishment. "Please," he said. "Don't do this. We have already agreed on this."

"Sorry," she said, clearly not the least bit sorry. "You just can't have it."

"Why not?" he asked. "It's all I'll have to get around in."

"Too bad," she said. "When all the children are in from school at the same time, we'll be short a car. I just need it."

"For Christ's sake," he said. "You've gotten everything else."

"You've still got your whore."

Oh, shit, I said (to myself), there goes the settlement.

There was silence in the room. My client looked at me for a good long time, obviously thinking the situation over. Then without a word he stood and climbed onto his chair. He stepped to the top of the conference room table. It was a big table, shiny mahogany, with at least sixteen chairs around it. We sat there, staring up at him, frozen. He walked to the middle of the table. He removed his pin-striped jacket—then his tie, then his shirt and pants, then his underwear. He turned and faced his wife. This was obviously not the first time he had stood before her in the nude, though not in front of others, and certainly not from that level. Then Mr. Jones cupped his hands aggressively around his testicles.

"The only thing I have left," Mr. Jones said to his wife, "are these. Do you want them, too?"

She took the Volkswagen.

He got the divorce.

ROBERT STEPHAN COHEN
MORRISON COHEN SINGER & WEINSTEIN, LLP
NEW YORK, NEW YORK

A Night of Bliss

ONE OF MY JOBS AS A ROOKIE ASSISTANT UNITED STATES attorney in Washington, D.C., was to review search warrant applications before they went to a judge for authorization. I would review them for legal sufficiency, so that if the judge did sign them and they were later challenged, they would hold up in court. Then I had to stay available by phone to the law enforcement officers who would serve and execute the warrants to assist them should any legal issues arise while they were performing their searches.

So when my phone rang I was not at all surprised to hear the voice of a sergeant on the narcotics squad calling directly from a suspect's apartment. The sergeant and his partner were in the middle of a search based on a warrant he had shown me earlier that morning. He told me they had a little problem down there. Well, here was my chance to show off all that legal knowledge I had absorbed (and my parents had paid for) in law school.

"What's the problem, Sergeant?" I asked, certain that I was about to dazzle this veteran policeman with my scholarly grasp of Constitutional principles of search and seizure. Or maybe, I thought, the sergeant was calling me because of some monumental mistake he and his partner had made—one that needed my expert legal analytical skills to resolve. The wrong apartment entered, perhaps, or the wrong guy caught? Maybe there were no drugs found, but some expensive stolen merchandise had been uncovered instead? You know, something like that.

But it was nothing at all like that.

It seems there were three people found in the apartment. The sergeant explained that three "perps" (cop talk for perpetrators) had been caught in the act of sorting and bagging some high-grade heroin.

"We got them down and dirty," the sergeant said, and they were going to be arrested on the spot.

"So?" I asked, still intrigued by what esoteric legal issue this search and arrest had triggered. It was obviously important enough, and complicated enough, for the sergeant to go to the trouble of phoning me right from the scene of the search—right from the perps' apartment.

"So what's the problem you-all got down there?" I asked again.

The problem, the sergeant said, was that they didn't know where to send the perps.

"Come again?" I said.

Well, it was like this, he said. Each of the three individuals was originally a male, but each was at a different stage of a sex-change operation. So the sergeant didn't know whether the arrested trio should be packed off to the D.C. jail or to the Women's Detention Center.

"What exactly do you mean by that?" I asked. It was at that point that I heard him place his hand over the receiver and say something to his partner, an observation in cop talk over what he took to be my inability to understand common simple English. Cops can be like that with young prosecutors. In any event, the sergeant explained what he meant.

He explained that two of the arrested perps had well-developed breasts. (He phrased it a little differently.) They also had equally well-developed penises. (I considered inquiring how exactly he knew that, but thought better of it.) The third perp's penis had already been removed, his breasts surgically enlarged, and ("get this," the sergeant had said), an artificial vagina had been surgically constructed. (Again, the sergeant said this in his own way.) So much for esoteric Fourth Amendment search-and-seizure questions. "So, Barcella," he asked, "what are we supposed to do down here?"

I mentally flipped through the catalogue of my law school curriculum for the answer the sergeant needed. Zero. So, receiver in hand, I tried something revolutionary for a lawyer. Common sense. Bingo.

"Okay, here's what you do," I instructed the sergeant. "Send the two guys with breasts to the D.C. jail. Send the guy with the vagina to the Women's Detention Center." The sergeant seemed satisfied and hung up. My boss, a straitlaced Irish Catholic, came into the office in time to hear only my instructions—he never looked at me as strangely as he did that day.

The next morning, I made it a point to go down to the Arraignment Court to explain to the prosecutor who would be processing the arrests from the day before what was going on with the three perps. A few minutes after I got to Arraignment Court, the three were led in from the cell block. The defendant that I had sent to the Women's Center—the perp with the vagina—was standing there apparently unconcerned about what was going on around him. But the other two defendants—the ones with both breasts and penises—whom I had sent to the D.C. jail, were a different story. I could easily see that they had spent a night of bliss. Both were beaming with a blush I had seen before only on newlyweds. They looked in my direction. I knew they had no idea who I was, or what role I'd played in arranging for their prior night's accommodations. Still, for just one brief moment I thought I could see looks of gratitude and appreciation in their starry eyes.

E. Lawrence Barcella, Jr.
Paul, Hastings, Janofsky & Walker LLP
Washington, D.C.

Disorder in the Court I

Here are some examples of transcripts of actual proceedings taken by court reporters showing what can happen when the subject turns to matters sexual. In the first case, the witness was probably claiming that he had lost sexual function as a result of some injury inflicted upon him for which he had sued for damages.

> QUESTION (THE LAWYER): Since the time—well, let me put it this way. Nowadays do you ever have trouble getting an erection?
> ANSWER (THE WITNESS): It's—it's harder than before.
> QUESTION: You mean harder to get one?
> ANSWER: No—right it's hard to get.
> QUESTION: It's more difficult?
> ANSWER: Yes.

Then there was the lawyer who just didn't get it.

> QUESTION: Do you know how far pregnant you are right now?
> ANSWER: I will be three months November 8.
> QUESTION: Apparently the date of conception was August 8?
> ANSWER: Yes.
> QUESTION: What were you and your husband doing at that time?

> QUESTION: When did you begin to plan your wedding?
> ANSWER: Well, actually, I didn't plan my wedding; my mother did.
> QUESTION: Did you participate in your mother's planning of your wedding?
> ANSWER: No. My mother is Italian.

QUESTION: When did your mother begin to plan your wedding?
ANSWER: When I was born.

QUESTION: Doctor, what treatment did you give this man?
ANSWER: I cleansed the wound, sutured it, and put him in bed with
a nurse.

Body Parts

FOR THE PAST EIGHTEEN YEARS I HAVE LABORED AS A SOLE practitioner in the great western town of Laramie, Wyoming. Folks out here sure get into some interesting legal troubles.

A Girl's Gotta Do What a Girl's Gotta Do

My client, a prostitute, and I were driving to Rawlins, Wyoming, a hundred miles west of Laramie, for her change of plea on a burglary charge. This was early in my practice and I hadn't learned yet to get retainers, and thought the drive presented an opportunity to discuss her failure to make payment on her substantial bill. She repeatedly promised me that she would pay my bill as soon as she was able to return to work. To assure me of her income-earning potential, she detailed her sexual expertise, her satisfied customers, and her charges for her services. I managed to listen soberly and almost nonjudgmentally while she detailed unlikely sexual positions, educated me about fetishes and sexual preferences, compared penis sizes (demonstrating with her hands the size of one particular penis that would have strained the credulity of *Penthouse* Forum readers), and recommended uses for ice water that I had never contemplated. Finally, however, she described how one client, a well-known local businessman, paid her $100 to defecate on his face. "For God's sake," I blurted out, "you don't kiss him after that, do you?" "Of course not," she said, insulted. "What kind of a girl do you think I am?"

Dressed for Court

It was a major drug bust. Twenty-six individuals were charged with possession of marijuana. Twenty-five pled guilty. The twenty-sixth refused and demanded a trial. He was my client. My client turned up for his pretrial hearing wearing a T-shirt emblazoned with a large marijuana leaf and the words "Weeds of Wisdom." My client didn't learn his lesson: at trial during jury selection, the prosecutor asked the jury panel if any of them believed that marijuana should be legalized. Only two people raised their hands: the mayor of Laramie, who had been drawn for jury duty, and my client.

The trial was held in July—because of our mild summers, there is no air conditioning in the courtroom. I was wearing a white linen suit with a charcoal blouse. As the courtroom grew warmer during the proceedings, I took off my jacket. Unfortunately, I was wearing black underwear. The local public defender, who was observing the trial, in a loud stage whisper, hissed, "Galvan, put your jacket on—we can see your braaa-ssiere," drawing titters from the jury and the attention of the prosecutor in mid-question. As I fumbled to replace my jacket gracefully, the courtroom erupted in laughter: the prosecutor's fly was open with his shirttail peeping through. Mercifully, the judge called a recess.

My client was acquitted: probably a sympathy vote for me.

The Scent of a Woman

An otherwise qualified young woman was denied employment on a seismographic crew for the stated business reason that "menstruation would attract bears." We sued.

The defendant's expert witness was the chief scientist at Glacier National Park, who testified to various experiments with brown bears, to see how they reacted to, among other things, dead fish and used tampons. His testimony was necessarily recessed when the president of the defendant company broke into hysterical laughter and fell over backward in his chair when I asked his expert, "And, sir, where did you get the used tampons?," eliciting the response "I don't know. From women, I guess."

The federal judge who was assigned the case is locally famous for his no-nonsense approach and his Wyoming chauvinism. Defense counsel were suave, debonair, and from Denver, Colorado. Already disgruntled by defense counsels' repeated complaints during the proceedings that "that's not the way we do things in Colorado," the judge asked them where the seismographic operations took place. They replied, In the vicinity of Cokesville, Wyoming. After considering the reply during a long moment's silence, the judge agreed. "Hmm, well, there may have been a bear there once—*in a circus!*"

We settled the case favorably.

(By the way, as far as I know, there is only one documented case of a menstruating woman who has been killed by a bear, in 1967 in Glacier National Park. The bear killed her dog and chased a male companion up a tree before turning on her.)

MARY ELIZABETH GALVAN
ATTORNEY AT LAW
LARAMIE, WYOMING

The Sobriety Test

I HAD A CASE IN A SMALL MIDWESTERN TOWN. MY CLIENTS were a newlywed couple. It seems that, as a wedding present, Daddy, a prominent local businessman, had given his darling daughter and her husband several million dollars' worth of stock. The couple then turned the investment portfolio over to a friend of theirs who had just become a stockbroker. He was so inept that it took him no time at all to lose everything. We sued the brokerage firm for whom the friend worked, alleging insufficient supervision of its negligent employee.

During the discovery phase of the case, the daughter's deposition was taken. Her husband did not attend her deposition. Her questioning was routine, pretty much what I expected. She was asked about the brokerage account and a series of bland questions about what instructions were given to the stockbroker, her husband's involvement in making investment decisions, etc., etc. As I said, routine questions, nothing unexpected. Then out of the blue, the brokerage firm's lawyer asked my client a curious question:

"Do you remember being out on Old Route 29 last New Year's Eve?"

I sat there wondering what on earth driving along Old Route 29 had to do with a securities case, but said nothing at the time, figuring I would let the lawyer proceed, for a short while anyway. The next series of questions were even more curious:

QUESTION: Was your husband with you?
ANSWER: No, I was alone.
QUESTION: Do you remember being stopped by Deputy Jones on that night?
ANSWER: Yes.
QUESTION: Do you recall being given a sobriety test?
ANSWER: Yes.

It was at this point that I thought I detected some discomfort on the part of my client. But the questioning seemed harmless enough. I figured that if the lawyer wanted to waste his time asking my client about some minor driving offense, rather than attempting to establish that the stockbroker was operating under instructions from his clients, or anything else that would help him defend his case, I would just let him go on. The next few questions, however, revealed his strategy:

QUESTION: Did you get a ticket?
ANSWER: No.
QUESTION: Why not?

What I expected to hear was my client informing the lawyer that she didn't get a ticket because she had passed the sobriety test. What I heard instead was my client bursting into tears. And what I felt was the pain in my shin where my client had delivered a sharp under-the-table kick.

Not being a total idiot, I requested a halt to the deposition to allow my client time to compose herself and took her out into the hall. The very instant the door to the deposition room closed behind us, her tears instantly stopped. My client looked me directly in the eye.

"Don't you dare let him ask me one more question about that," she said, her tone leaving no doubt that this was not a debatable subject. Nevertheless, I suppose to make absolutely clear to me what my instructions were, my client added, "You got that?"

I told her I did and we then reentered the deposition room. Once inside, I refused to permit any further questioning on that subject.

I never asked her what happened that evening out on Old Route 29. I didn't need to.

And would you believe it, her husband decided to drop the case the day after his wife's deposition. He called and told me that his wife simply couldn't bear the thought of harming their good friend the young stockbroker.

I told him I completely understood.

FRANK C. RAZZANO
DICKSTEIN SHAPIRO MORIN & OSHINSKY LLP
WASHINGTON, D.C.

The Price of Beauty

JOHN PATRICK O'BRIEN SERVED FOR MANY YEARS AS A JUDGE of the Common Pleas Court in the city of Detroit. Harold Ryan served as his courtroom clerk.

Early in my career I was representing the city of Detroit's municipal bus company, defending a case where a car that was double-parked in the "red light" district suddenly pulled forward as our bus passed and caused damage to it.

In cross-examining the driver of the car, I asked whether his car had been stopped immediately before the impact. He replied that it had.

I then asked what he had been doing at the time. His reply was that he was speaking to a woman who had stopped him on the sidewalk. I asked whether she was beautiful. His reply was to the effect that he couldn't tell me whether she was beautiful, since everyone had his or her own view of the subject.

I asked the nature of their discussion.

He replied that she was seeking a loan. I asked him how much that "loan" was for.

He replied, "Twenty dollars." At that point, Judge O'Brien leaned down to his clerk and said in a stage whisper, "Harold, she wasn't very beautiful."

JAMES R. KOHL
PLUNKETT & COONEY
BLOOMFIELD HILLS, MICHIGAN

Not a Pretty Picture

AFTER GRADUATING FROM LAW SCHOOL, I WORKED AS A LAW clerk to a federal judge. While I was there, the judge tried a variety of cases. Among the ones I'll never forget was a pornography case involving someone charged with using the U.S. mails to distribute allegedly pornographic magazines. I say "allegedly" for two reasons.

First, this occurred in the days before most neighborhood video stores' back rooms were loaded with shelves for rental of explicitly graphic XXX tapes. You see, the magazines at issue were what is called "soft porn." The photographs were of nude men and women, in really close proximity to one another, but never actually touching. And although these "models" were lasciviously leering at one another, clearly suggesting to the viewer what was on their minds, the men were not erect, and the women—well, to tell you the truth all I can really remember about the women was how unattractive they were.

The second reason for use of the word *allegedly* is that the defendant was acquitted. While I never discussed it with the judge, I always thought the pig had something to do with how the case turned out.

And no, I'm not referring to a particularly unattractive female model in one of the magazines. An actual pig *was* involved in the case. Well, a picture of a pig. A series of pictures—kind of a storyboard, if you could call what the pig and the female model did a story.

In order to convince the judge that his client's magazines weren't really so bad, the defense lawyer cleverly put into evidence a group of sexually explicit magazines acquired in Denmark, where all pornography was legal. His point was to show the judge what real pornography looked like, when compared with the soft porn contained in his client's magazines. These Danish magazines contained pictures of twosomes, threesomes, foursomes, you name it, all explicitly engaged in every form of sex act imaginable. The final exhibit offered by the defense lawyer was the magazine containing the woman and the pig.

The first picture showed the woman walking into the barn. There she sees the pig, minding his own business, standing in his stall, chewing his cud, or whatever it is that pigs do when they're alone in their stalls. Then, for reasons I suppose must be untranslatable from the Danish, the woman becomes sexually aroused by the sight of the pig. (Go figure?) Anyway, this is followed by a series of pictures, pig prominently shown in the background, while the woman starts rubbing herself, and then shedding her dress—revealing, of course, fire engine red panties and garters, what every farm girl wears when entering a barn. And then, without further ado, the remainder of the magazine contains photos of the woman and the pig locked in the amorous embrace of the sex act. The final picture shows the woman assisting the pig in securing its release. (No, *not* from the barn! You know what I mean.)

The comparison worked. After viewing the Danish pornography, the judge acquitted the defendant of all charges. In writing his opinion, however, the judge simply could not let go the disdain he felt for those who had permitted themselves to be photographed in the most private of acts. The only participant for whom he cut some slack was the pig. Here's what he wrote:

> Defendants also marked for identification a magazine containing photographs of bestiality. To his everlasting credit may it be said that the [pig] was the only participant evidencing any signs of reluctance or embarrassment. (*United States v. Boltansky,* opinion of the Honorable R. Dorsey Watkins.)

R.L.

The Porn Queen

As far back as high school at the Convent of the Sacred Heart, I knew that I wanted to become a trademark lawyer like my father. I began my legal career at a small firm specializing in real estate and trusts and estates. But then I changed law firms and, within a year, I had become a full-time trademark lawyer, just like my dad. Well, not exactly just like my dad. He handled trademark issues representing sober and respectable commercial interests, while I became the Porn Queen. (What will the nuns back at the Convent of the Sacred Heart say now? Can I attend alumnae functions? What will my dad think?)

The Call

It all started slowly—snuck up on me, actually. A partner called. A new client, he said. An interesting trademark issue that he would like me to work on. But there was this strange silence on the other end of the line. There was something more to this. The partner was having trouble.

"Uhm," he said.

I waited.

"Uhm," he repeated.

"Yes?" I said, expectantly.

"The thing is . . ." he said. Then he paused again. More silence. I heard him clear his throat. "Thing is, the work involves . . . well, it involves registering a client's Internet domain names, and well, there . . . you know . . . there . . . uhm."

Uhm again, I thought. What is this? What's he trying to tell me?

"Uhm," the partner said for the umpteenth time.

The partner mumbled something into his mouthpiece.

"Corn?" I asked, wondering, does he want me to work on some sort of farming cooperative Internet Web site?

"Corn?" the partner repeated, confused.

We were clearly going nowhere fast. I told him that I thought he had said corn. Another pause. Then he grabbed the bull by the horns, so to speak, and explained my new assignment.

I was to assist in the registering of a series of domain names that contained what is customarily called adult entertainment.

"Oh, porn!" I said, almost shouting into the phone. My relief at finally figuring out what the partner was trying to tell me was that great.

"Yes, that's right," the partner said, hurriedly adding that the new case file materials would be arriving on my desk shortly. He seemed quite eager to get off this call.

Picture This

I was actually excited about the new project. Registering porn domain names as trademarks was going to be a challenge. In order properly to represent one's client and to file trademark applications, the lawyer needs to understand as much as possible about the client's business and the products or services under which their trademarks are being used. Therefore, with this project I had no choice but to log onto the Internet and check out these domain names and the porn sites they connected to. Honest. (Really, Sister Theresa, I had no choice. Dad, you're with me on this one, aren't you?)

This is when the rest of my office got interested in what I was doing. I started with "www.porn.com." Within seconds I had more on my screen than I bargained for and couldn't help but wonder what anyone who looked over my shoulder would think. I mean, you can't believe what was flashing across my screen!

I found myself casually mentioning the subject matter wherever I could, alerting everyone to the fact that this was strictly billable time. This is when I noticed that my colleagues and staff were becoming interested and wanted to help me: secretaries offered to type . . . other associates asked if I needed help researching, even some of the partners asked if I needed any guidance or input.

There's No Business Like Show Business

I must have done a good job. It didn't take long for me to receive another project. And then another. And then another.

One of my biggest adult entertainment projects came from our insolvency department. It began with another phone call, this time from another associate.

"I was instructed to call you by the partner who heads our insolvency department," the associate said.

"But I'm in our trademark section," I said, now worried that the firm was going to send me out of trademarks and into another practice area.

"Yep," the associate said. "You're the Porn Queen."

Shortly thereafter I received a list of trademarks. They were for a string of magazines. Each magazine contained a title containing a series of adjectives describing the activities, physical attributes, or intentions of the young men and women depicted in the photographs inside their pages. Adjectives like hot, juicy, naughty, wet . . . you get the picture. At first I thought this was some kind of joke. I called the associate back and asked what was going on. The associate seemed embarrassed. Apologetically, she explained that the firm represented a bankrupt publishing company. A bankrupt porn publishing company.

"Welcome to the PPG," she said.

"To the what?" I said.

"The PPG," she repeated. "The Porn Practice Group."

She went on to explain that ever since the insolvency section had undertaken the representation of the bankrupt porn publisher, the partner in charge had given that name to their efforts. "You were a natural to join us," the associate added. "Given your reputation and all."

Interestingly, the group was made up of a male partner and three women associates. I quickly became the Porn Queen of that group, too, although there were several male attorneys who expressed a strong interest in joining the group. They too wanted to traverse the Internet porn sites on the client's time.

The ultimate success of the PPG came when the magazine business was sold out of the bankrupt estate. The new owners promptly hired us to represent them. I was placed in charge of over thirty-five porn trademarks in various stages of registration, and a client that wanted to expand to the Internet quickly.

Porn brings up a lot of cutting-edge legal issues. I deal with First Amendment rights, domain name issues, trademark "immoral and scandalous" issues, infringement issues, copyright issues, and even possible patent issues for protecting business methods.

But I'm sick of the pictures!

And I realize that Sister Theresa is unlikely to ask me to speak at the alumnae reunion.

As it turns out, I left the firm for another job, a quiet existence as in-house counsel to a major corporation. Although becoming the Porn Queen was clearly not my goal when I went to law school, I bet it would have gotten me a partnership had I stayed.

SUSAN M. DALY
TRADEMARK COUNSEL
SUNBEAM CORPORATION
BOCA RATON, FLORIDA

Why Do They Do What They Do?

I USED TO DO MORE DOMESTIC RELATIONS WORK THAN I DO now. Here's why.

Case 1

I got a call from opposing counsel in a hotly contested divorce case. He got right to the point. "Jim, I've got a tape recording you've got to hear," he said. A day or two later I went to his office.

He explained that my female client had been involved in an adulterous affair with a man who lived next door, that the fellow had begun to feel guilty because he knew the husband as well, and so had gone to the lawyer. For some reason, the man had taped an episode of their lovemaking. He had hidden the recorder under the couch before my client came to pay a visit one morning. The lawyer then played the tape.

The recording was scratchy, partly inaudible, but generally the action could be pretty well understood. Especially when the man said, "I've got some whipped cream in the refrigerator. I'll go get it if you'll lick it off my_____."

The tape was about twelve minutes in length, but the clincher came at the end when, after some unidentifiable sound in the distance, the action quieted down and a little voice said, "Mommy, what are you doing?"

It seems my client's small daughter, wondering where her mother had gone, decided to look next door.

Case 2

In a not too dissimilar situation, another friendly lawyer called and said, "I've got something for you to see." Again, I went.

When I sat down in his conference room, he dumped a large manila envelope of photographs on the table. In this divorce, I represented the man who was featured in each picture. Although he wore dozens of different pieces of clothing (mostly lingerie), my client usually had on a bra (clearly stuffed with something) and panties (which mostly revealed his masculinity). He even wore high heels and, yes, lipstick.

The other lawyer explained that the wife had found the pictures in an old bureau and confirmed that the snapshots had been taken in the attic of their home. She believed he had a time-set camera mounted on a tripod and so had snapped the pictures himself.

As best I can remember, cross-dressing was never per se grounds for divorce; although to judge from those pictures, it probably qualifies as mental cruelty. In any event, my client was a doctor; the humiliation quotient was high. The case never went to trial.

Case 3

My secretary handed me the phone.

"One of your clients. Sounds urgent."

"What's up?" I asked my client, a civilian employee at a military base here in Dayton, Ohio.

He said he had taken ill at work and had gone home early. He parked in his garage and walked into his house in time to see his completely nude wife running down the hall into their bedroom, slamming the door behind her. He tried the door. Locked. He demanded entry. Silence. By the time he managed to break through, there was his wife, dressing in the corner, seemingly alone.

"Hi. Home early?" she asked, as though nothing at all unusual had just happened.

For a moment he actually believed that nothing was wrong. Maybe it was his illness playing tricks on him, he thought. But then he saw a pair of man's trousers—not his—lying partially beneath the bed.

My client walked to the closet while his wife continued dressing. He thought he could tell she was watching him closely, although she seemed not to be the least bit concerned. He opened the closet door and there beneath the hanging clothes he saw a pair of hairy legs. As he brushed aside the clothes, the man attached to the hairy legs hit him. My client fell backward, temporarily stunned. The man and my client's wife then took off on a dead run. My client ran to the window in time to see them leaving the driveway. In *his* car.

About an hour later, he heard his car returning to the garage. His wife walked up the stairs whistling a little tune.

"Who the hell was that guy?" my client demanded.

"What guy?" she said.

So, as I said, I don't handle many domestic relations cases these days.

JAMES E. CROSS
ALLBERY CROSS FOGARTY
DAYTON, OHIO

Keeping Abreast of the Law

MY LAW OFFICE HAD BEEN OPEN ONLY TWO WEEKS WHEN A friend referred an entire family that had been injured in an automobile accident—grandmother, mother, and two daughters. In my cramped office, all four of them sat across from me at my desk. I carefully questioned each one of my new clients to determine the nature and extent of their injuries, making precise notes on my yellow legal pad, using the brand-new Mont Blanc fountain pen my wife had given me as a good-luck present.

As I questioned the grandmother, who sat directly across from me, she explained that she had hit her chest on the dashboard of the automobile and that she had sustained very bad bruising. As I was carefully writing all this down, she suddenly opened her dress and flopped one colossal breast across my desk. It fell right onto my legal pad, covering the very words I had just written, smudging the still-wet ink. She let her breast rest right where it had landed.

"You see?" she said, indicating that a closer look was in order.

I looked.

In fact, I looked so hard, I seemingly lost track of time. Like the rest of her family, the grandmother was a beautiful shade of ebony. Her huge breast was right there, directly in my line of vision. I saw skin, opaque and soft, a massive dark nipple, and sure enough, spreading like some purplish river across a dark continent, the bruise in question. All this color was accentuated by the pale yellow of my legal pad, itself covered with the bright-blue ink of my old-fashioned fountain pen. Then I realized that some of the blue had transferred itself onto the woman's breast. Instinctively, I reached into my pocket for my handkerchief, thinking—well, I suppose I was doing a little less thinking here—that maybe I could wipe off some of that ink before it had completely dried. Just as my hand reached my pocket, I heard a voice way off in the distance. Slowly, I realized that the voice actually was quite close at hand and it belonged to the mother.

"Mama," she was saying, "now, you put that away and let the man work."

As I watched the grandmother fold her breast back into her dress, I saw the ink spot. By this time I had retrieved my hankie and with one quick swipe I could have . . . But I let it go. Grandma nodded at me. There, she seemed to be saying. Now you see?

Well, we settled the case. The other driver's insurance company paid the policy limits. And while it wasn't really a lot of money, my share of the proceeds allowed me to remain in practice.

I have a larger office these days.

Less client contact.

NORMAN L. SLOAN
HORTON, SLOAN & GERBER, PLLC
WINSTON-SALEM, NORTH CAROLINA

Shell-Shocked

My client had been charged with the crime of exposing himself to a minor. He was a school bus driver who had allegedly displayed his penis to a little girl who had just gotten on the bus. He claimed he was innocent. His defense: that he was merely adjusting himself when the girl stepped onto the bus and happened to see him.

On the second day of trial, when my client and I arrived in the courtroom, the spectator section was packed with high school students. It seems their teacher had arranged with the judge for them to spend the day in court as a sort of workshop civics lesson. I learned that about half of the kids were French foreign exchange students. While they spoke English, it was far from perfect.

Before the day's testimony began, the judge outlined the case for the students, explaining that if my client was convicted, he could be sentenced up to one year in jail.

I later learned that the French students were shocked by the severity of the American judicial system. At the classroom discussion that occurred the following day, one of the French kids said it was appalling that a judge would give a man a year in jail just for showing his *peanuts* to a child.

JERRY BERRY
BERRY, DAY & McFEE
NAPLES, FLORIDA

Dated

SHORTLY AFTER I HAD BECOME ENGAGED TO MY WIFE, I finished a major real estate closing at a downtown Miami law office. As I was walking toward the exit, feeling on top of the world, one of the secretaries, a striking brunette, looked up from her desk and asked, "Do you want to go out?" I was stunned. Never, when I was single, had a woman so brazenly asked me this question. Clearly, my lawyerly qualities were apparent to all.

As I stood silently, wondering why this had to happen only after I had become engaged, she again asked, "Do you want to go out?" As I stumbled for an answer, she stood up, pointed her finger, and said, "The door is over there." My ego, having been sufficiently deflated, allowed me to mumble a quick goodbye and I left.

MARSHALL J. EMAS
ENGLISH, MCCAUGHAN & O'BRYAN, P.A.
FORT LAUDERDALE, FLORIDA

Calling Dr. Freud

In Saudi Arabia, women are permitted to work in only a few reserved occupations, primarily in the field of medical care. All other positions—business executive, doctor, lawyer—are occupied by males. Even secretaries working in offices are male and usually are either Indian or Pakistani Muslims with orthodox views on the appropriateness of women in the workplace. But as I am about to relate, like all God's creatures, they are human, too.

Some years ago, the firm of London solicitors for which I then worked had need for some additional lawyers to staff its branch office in Jeddah. It seemed as though the experience would be interesting from both a legal and cultural point of view, so I volunteered to go.

While there, I did some legal work for the Saudi subsidiary of an offshore bank. Interestingly, this bank employed one of the very few (perhaps the only) female banking officers in the entire country. Needless to say, the bank was understandably discreet about the employment of the lady concerned, who worked in an office resembling a broom closet. And though she kept her head covered at all times, as both tradition and local law required, she was noticeably quite attractive. On a few occasions we had meetings in my office, where my male secretary would have occasion to see her.

On one of these occasions I provided some legal advice to her, which I thought was of too small a nature to deserve a bill for services rendered. So after the woman left my office, I dictated a letter to my secretary advising that I would not be forwarding an invoice to her. I remember that on that afternoon when my secretary presented me with my dictated letters for signature, I was in a bit of a rush. I am ashamed to admit that the most mundane letters escaped an exacting review.

The next day I had a chance to review my file copies of the letters sent the day before. My secretary had typed the first portion of my letter to the lady as follows:

"Dear [   ]: In case you are awaiting with *baited breasts* for my invoice for legal services . . ."

I phoned the woman and apologized. I decided not to mention the letter to my secretary.

I doubt he had ever heard of Dr. Freud.

SIMON BUCKINGHAM
TRAVERS SMITH BRAITHWAITE
LONDON, ENGLAND

One More Question

T HE FOLLOWING STORY WAS RELATED TO ME BY THE LAWYER involved:

The divorce case was fiercely contested in a trial that lasted several days. Husband and wife really went at it. Each of them had taken the witness stand and made horrible, scurrilous accusations against the other, ranging from felonies to conduct that was merely awful. At the conclusion of the trial, the judge rendered his decision. While neither party came out the clear winner, the wife did marginally better than the husband.

As the lawyers were packing up their papers to leave the courtroom, the husband, still seated at counsel's table, is reported to have said to the wife, "Honey, come over here a minute, I want to ask you something."

Armed with her purse in hand, the wife cautiously walked over to where her husband was seated, when he said, "I suppose a blow job would be out of the question?" The wife swung her purse in a powerful arc, knocking off his glasses and putting a sizable gash in his forehead.

He said it was worth it.

JOHN C. EVERETT
EVERETT LAW FIRM
FAYETTEVILLE, ARKANSAS

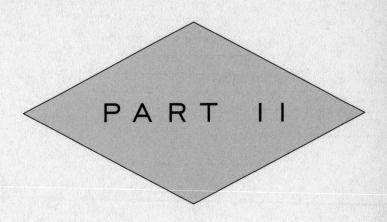

PART II

WITNESS THE WITNESS

T HE COURTROOM IS PACKED. THE CAMERA SWINGS ALONG THE benches, capturing the faces of those who have come to watch this most momentous of cases. The prosecutor has just announced to the judge with obvious satisfaction, "No more questions, Your Honor." The defense attorney ponderously rises from his seat at counsel's table. The whole trial rests on the skill of his cross-examination of this, the state's key witness. In older shows, the defense attorney is Perry Mason and the TV picture is in black and white. In other, more recent shows, it's some other famous fictional defense attorney and the picture is in color. But it really doesn't matter, the high drama is the same.

The witness is the defendant's wife, sometimes his lover, or on occasion his former business partner. The TV camera captures her (or him) sitting just slightly back in the witness chair. There's a smirk running across her (or his) lips. The first series of questions from Perry Mason have missed their mark. He hasn't laid a glove on the witness. This is going to be easy, the witness can be seen thinking. Hey, I'm like smarter than this fancy-pants lawyer who's been the hero of four years' worth of successful one-hour episodes—winning every case in the last five minutes of each show. Perry seems to be stumbling. The camera once again pans the full-to-capacity courtroom. You can see by the looks on their faces as well, the general thinking here is that Perry is going to blow this one. His innocent but unjustly accused client is going down the chute. Life in prison without possibility of parole. Maybe some sordid experiences of prison gang rape, or other violent acts await him (or her). This looks really bad.

But then, guess what? Perry comes to life. With the camera zooming in on his stern yet wise face, Perry begins a series of questions that will cut like a knife through the heart of the witness's pack of lies.

"Now, I ask you, Mrs. (or Mr.) Jones, isn't it a fact that . . ."

And so on. The camera catches the witness, no longer relaxed in the box, leaning uncomfortably forward, the smirk gone, replaced first with a frown, then a nervous tic.

"And isn't it also a fact that . . ."

Before too long (certainly before the last set of commercials), the witness is done in; she (or he) blurts out for all the courtroom to hear that, no, Perry's client didn't commit the heinous murder for which he is standing trial.

"I did it! I did it!" the witness screams, now hysterical, completely broken by Perry's expertly handled, brilliant cross-examination. The witness sobs the remainder of the necessary confession. The camera captures the relief on the defendant's face, then focuses on Perry's look of deep and sincere sorrow for the fate of this poor unfortunate witness who will now be sent to the gallows. The last shot is of the audience, who collectively can be seen satisfied that justice will now be done, thanks of course to the lawyer's skillful cross-examination of the witness.

And that is what we expect in real life. Well, as this chapter will reveal, questioning of witnesses rarely, if ever, yields the melodrama and picture-perfect results that Perry Mason and his TV successors achieved week in and week out. On the other hand, there have been some wonderful experiences between witnesses and the lawyers assigned to question them.

Let's begin with actual transcripts. Then we'll go to stories contributed by lawyers containing real episodes of some of their most memorable experiences.

Disorder in the Court II

QUESTION: What is your brother-in-law's name?
ANSWER: Borofkin.
QUESTION: What is his first name?
ANSWER: I can't remember.
QUESTION: He's been your brother-in-law for forty-five years and you can't remember his name?
ANSWER: No, I tell you I'm too excited. [Rising from the witness chair and pointing to Mr. Borofkin]: Nathan, for God's sake, tell them your first name!

QUESTION: Trooper, was the defendant obviously drunk when you arrested her?
DEFENSE COUNSEL: Objection, Your Honor. It calls for a conclusion.
THE COURT: Sustained.
QUESTION: Trooper, when you stopped the defendant were your red and blue lights flashing?
ANSWER: Yes, sir.
QUESTION: Did the defendant say anything when she got out of her car?
ANSWER: Yes, sir.
QUESTION: What did she say?
ANSWER: "What disco am I at?"

QUESTION: Do you recall approximately the time that you examined the body of Mr. Edgington at the Rose Chapel?

ANSWER: It was in the evening. The autopsy started about 8:30 P.M.

QUESTION: And Mr. Edgington was dead at that time, is that correct?

ANSWER: No, you dumb asshole. He was sitting there on the table wondering why I was doing an autopsy.

Old Man Peveto's Mule

I WAS BORN AND RAISED IN DEEP EAST TEXAS AND HAVE LIVED in Beaumont, Texas, most of my life. Beaumont is a medium-sized Texas town, with shopping malls and a downtown area. But the outlying district can be quite rural. The case I had years ago involved Old Man Peveto. He has a first and middle name, but pretty much everyone just called him Old Man Peveto. Anyway, the case took place in one of the most rural and desolate spots in the county.

It seems that Old Man Peveto was driving his pickup truck from his country road onto the main road just as my client's delivery truck came along. My client's truck couldn't stop in time and hit Old Man Peveto in the rear, injuring him severely. But that wasn't all. Peveto had his mule tied to the back of his pickup at the time, pulling it along as he went. The mule was killed. Peveto sued.

Our defense was that Old Man Peveto pulled from the side road directly into the path of the truck without so much as a sideways glance, thereby causing the accident. He, of course, denied this, claiming that when he pulled onto the main road, there was no vehicle in sight. Then, from out of nowhere, came my client's delivery truck racing down the road with the speed of a bullet. The mule saw it first and whinnied, causing Peveto to turn and see what was the matter. By then it was too late. He tried swerving to the right, but the accident was unavoidable. He loved that mule, he added in his deposition, implying that life wouldn't be the same without it.

So it looked like the case would be my client's word against that of Old Man Peveto, up to the jury to decide which of the two they believed. But then I learned the accident might have had a witness, an old country boy who lived in a shack back up in the woods near the site of this unfortunate occurrence. I got the sheriff to do some investigating for me and, sure enough, he found our witness.

I drove on over to the area. That is, I drove as far into the area as I could. Our witness had no phone, no postal address, and no road up to his place. The sheriff had given me directions, so I was pretty sure I could find it. And sure enough, about half a mile down this worn path I came upon my man, sitting outside at an old table, drinking milk from a wooden bowl. A second bowl sat on the table. A chicken was drinking milk out of that one.

I introduced myself and was told to sit a spell if I was going to visit. As I sat down he invited me to have some milk with him, telling me that I needn't worry, the milk was fresh because he had gotten it straight from the cow less than five minutes ago and if I wanted some I best shoo that chicken away from the other bowl. I gracefully declined his offer and discussed the accident with him instead.

The fellow confirmed that the accident had happened just as the driver of my client's delivery truck said it had. We chatted for a while longer, mostly about the weather and its likely effect on the crops that year, and then I left. Later, I got the sheriff to serve him with a subpoena and explain to him that he had to be in court and when he had to be there. In fact, the sheriff saw to it that he was in court on the morning of the trial.

The trial was in January and it was very cold. I said that the sheriff saw to it that our witness was in court that morning and he was. But he stood there in the courthouse lobby barefoot. I didn't want my star witness going on the stand barefoot so I gave him some money to buy a pair of shoes. But I forgot to tell him to buy socks too.

When he took the stand later that morning it was obvious that shoes were not something he was terribly familiar with—and since his pants were well above his shoes, the jury could see he was sockless.

He was sworn in without difficulty. I then took him on direct examination, asking him what he saw, and he repeated what he had told me when I had visited with him back there in the woods at his house. The other lawyer then took him on cross-examination.

It seems that our witness knew Old Man Peveto and didn't much care for him. The lawyer tried to make something of that, implying with his questions that the witness had a motive for lying. At one point the lawyer asked him if he wasn't voluntarily appearing in court just to get Old Man Peveto in trouble.

"No, sir," the witness said, pulling his copy of the subpoena out of his overalls and explaining that the piece of paper was why he was there.

"Can you read that subpoena?" the lawyer asked, confident of the answer he would get.

"No, sir," the witness said again, explaining that he could neither read nor write, but he didn't have to, because the sheriff came and told him he had to come.

He then told the lawyer that he might not be educated like he was, but he didn't have to be because he knew what he saw.

"Now, sir," he said, "I know what a mule looks like. Know what a truck looks like." He then pointed over to where Old Man Peveto was seated. "Know what Old Man Peveto looks like, too," he said, adding, "and I seen Old Man Peveto pull out right in front of that big truck."

The attorney then began to ask him about things I might have told him and the witness promptly replied, "That man didn't want me to do nothing but tell the truth and you remember you tried to get me to lie when you talked to me."

The witness had the jury in stitches. Finally, the attorney asked the witness how he could be so absolutely certain of what he claimed to have seen.

"Now, look here," the witness said, "I done told you time and again, I seen Old Man Peveto and his mule pull right out in front of that truck. Now, I know Old Man Peveto ain't too smart, but that mule of his should of knowed better than to do that."

The jury believed the witness and found accordingly.

GILBERT I. "BUDDY" LOW
ORGAIN, BELL & TUCKER, L.L.P.
BEAUMONT, TEXAS

The Witness

SOUTHWESTERN LOUISIANA WAS SETTLED BY THE ACADIANS (more commonly known to fans of Paul Prudhomme's cooking as Cajuns) after their forced exodus from Nova Scotia. In many rural areas of the region Cajun French is not only a commonly heard language, it is often the *only* language spoken by the residents. As is true of any bilingual society, court proceedings often require translators to allow every participant in a trial a full understanding of what is being said, as well as to ensure a true record of the proceedings. This procedure usually does not cause much difficulty, since many of the judges (being elected officials in French-speaking territory) speak the language, as do their court reporters. The same is not true of many lawyers who travel to the small towns to defend suits filed by the local residents against large corporations. Most of these lawyers come from larger cities, since representing big corporations is not conducive to a prosperous practice in most small Louisiana towns.

Such an out-of-town lawyer, whom we'll call Frank, hailing from the city of New Orleans, once traveled to Ville Platte, Louisiana, to defend a railroad in a suit arising out of a collision between a car and a train at a railroad crossing. A local man, Gaston Robichaux, had in the early evening attempted—without success—to beat a freight train to the crossing. Mr. Robichaux's lawyer claimed that the train was speeding, failed to signal, and didn't stop when it could have, before injuring poor Mr. Robichaux. The only eyewitness to the accident was Placide Domingue, a farmer whose home was near the crossing in question. Placide did not speak any English, and thus required the services of the court reporter to translate Placide's answers to the lawyers' questions.

This procedure worked smoothly during direct examination by Aristide Soileau, Mr. Robichaux's local lawyer, who, of course, spoke Cajun French. The lawyer would pose his questions in French, the court reporter would translate for the benefit of Frank, then the witness would answer in French, followed by a translation into English. Frank became more frustrated by the minute, since both the witness and the local lawyer, as well as the judge and everyone else in the courtroom, understood what was being said and therefore didn't have to wait for the translations.

Placide related his story, telling the court that he had witnessed the accident, that the train never signaled and hit Gaston's car at a high rate of speed. Placide's testimony was becoming more and more damaging to the railroad, especially since the jury members and other spectators could easily follow the testimony as it was given, rather than having to wait for the English translations as Frank did. Finally, Placide finished his account and Frank began to cross-examine.

The language barrier between Frank and the witness Placide made cross-examination even more difficult than usual. In addition Frank seemed unable to get Placide to waver from his story of the speeding train crushing the helpless Gaston at the crossing. Like many lawyers who can't shake a witness's story, Frank began resorting to efforts to trip Placide on small details, hoping to cast doubt on Placide's ability to remember all details of an accident that had occurred several years earlier. Placide was asked such questions as where he was sitting when he saw the accident and whether there were any trees or other obstructions blocking his view of the train crossing. Also, like many lawyers, Frank asked these questions in several different ways, each question requiring the slow dance of translation of the question and response. Placide became more impatient by the minute, but Frank kept droning on.

Finally, in apparent desperation, Frank, through the translator, asked Placide where the sun was situated at the time of the accident, apparently hoping Placide would be unable to remember. The translator duly related this question to Placide, who, becoming agitated, launched into a long speech in French, with much gesticulation and exclamations. When Placide finally finished, the reporter turned to Frank and said, "He says the sun was in the west."

Frank, realizing that Placide must have said more than what was being reported, indignantly insisted upon a full translation. The judge responded by telling Frank that the best summary of Placide's answer was as reported, "in the west." Frank pressed his objection, demanding a full translation of Placide's answer. Finally, the judge, recognizing that an appellate court would someday review the record (one where the judges didn't have to speak French to get elected), agreed to provide a full translation, as follows:

"Sir, Placide says that he has no interest in this case, and is here only because he was summoned by the sheriff to come. Placide has a crop in the field next to this railroad crossing, and wishes very much to be done with this proceeding so that he can tend to his crop. He says that he has patiently tried to answer all of your picayune questions about the speed of the train, the sound of whistles, the height and shape of trees, and the like. But when you ask him where the sun would be at five P.M., when every fool knows it is in the west every day, without fail, he must consider you to be not only a fool, but a damn fool."

The railroad settled the case.

ROBERT L. CABES
MILLING BENSON WOODWARD L.L.P.
LAFAYETTE, LOUISIANA

The Speed of Light

I WAS A CIRCUIT COURT JUDGE FOR A NUMBER OF YEARS IN Davidson County, Tennessee. On one occasion I heard an appeal from a speeding ticket based on a radar gun. The issue before me was whether a radar gun was a reliable instrument for determining speed. The city attorney produced an expert employed by the manufacturer of the radar gun, who brought with him to the witness stand one of the radar guns and proceeded to demonstrate it. The expert testified that this radar gun was a marvelous piece of technology. In fact, it was fail-safe. It could be calibrated by use of a tuning fork and once calibrated was absolutely reliable. He testified that its operation was so simple that no once could mess it up. For example, if the battery was weak, it would go blank. If more than one target presented itself, it would go blank. If anything else that could possibly go wrong happened, it would simply go blank.

While he was giving this explanation, I was up on the bench playing with the radar gun. The lawyer for the defendant who was contesting the ticket was an older gentleman who weighed about 300 pounds. As he ambled across the courtroom I aimed the radar gun at him and pulled the trigger.

I then turned to the expert on the witness stand and the dialogue went something like this:

COURT: Sir, let me be sure I understand your expert opinion. Are you saying that no matter the conditions, if a person points this radar gun, pulls the trigger, whatever number appears on the readout is going to be accurate, without a doubt?

EXPERT: That's absolutely right, Judge.

COURT: You're positive that whatever the gun was pointed at was going the speed shown on the readout?

EXPERT: Positive, Judge.

COURT: All right [showing the expert the readout], what is it in this
   courtroom that is going 87 miles per hour?

Sure enough, the readout on the radar gun was showing 87 mph.

The expert looked at me, then the gun, then over to the city attorney.
Then to me again.

"It's the fluorescent lighting," he said.

At that point the defense lawyer lumbered to his feet.

"Can't be, Judge," he said. "I've been watching them. The lights
haven't moved at all."

Case dismissed.

STEVE NORTH
NORTH LAW OFFICE
MADISON, TENNESSEE

Good as New

I HAD THE PLAINTIFF ON CROSS-EXAMINATION, AND HE TESTIFIED to a story made out of whole cloth. He was very much smarter than I was, and on cross-examination he was always two steps ahead of me and I could not make a dent in what he was saying. Finally, in desperation, I turned to him.

"Won't your conscience bother you," I asked, "for telling us a story made out of whole cloth?"

The plaintiff quickly responded without hesitation. "No," he said. "My conscience is as good as new—I have never used it."

SIDNEY BARROWS (1918–1998)
LEONARD, STREET AND DEINARD, P.A.
MINNEAPOLIS, MINNESOTA

The Truth, the Whole Truth, Nothing but the Truth

I WAS PREPARING A CLIENT FOR A DEPOSITION IN A PERSONAL injury case. I had given him the usual instructions about answering only the question that was asked, not volunteering information, and answering in as short a manner as possible. I felt good about his understanding of the instructions.

Midway through the deposition, the opposing counsel asked this question:

> OPPOSING COUNSEL: Have you ever been convicted of a felony?
> CLIENT: No. They were all misdemeanors.

Needless to say, we spent another hour on his criminal record.

STRATTON TAYLOR
TAYLOR, BURRAGE, FOSTER & SINGHAL
CLAREMORE, OKLAHOMA

Just Another Day
in Court

I WAS SITTING IN AN OLD COURTHOUSE IN A SMALL TOWN IN Michigan, waiting to be heard on a rather mundane motion and wishing for a distraction. A capacity crowd watched as the judge worked his way through an uninspiring docket of no-fault divorces and driver's license re-instatement petitions. The lawyer representing the state argued the license cases, one after the other, without even sitting down, the clerk calling them out in a bored tone, the judge disposing of them without fanfare. The whole exercise took on a tedious rhythm. I started counting the holes in the ceiling tiles.

The clerk called yet another license petition, and I kept counting. Then a lanky young man stood, walked toward the front of the courtroom, and looked nervously around. He started when the clerk called his name again.

"I'm here, Judge, but I don't think my lawyer is." He doesn't know what his lawyer looks like. Not a good sign.

Just then a burly little man in a rumpled tan suit pushes through the courtroom doors and, in a loud whisper, begins interrogating the people waiting in the pews.

"Are you Mr. Jones? Are you Mr. Jones? Ma'am, would you ask that gentleman if he's Mr. Jones? Is there a Mr. Jones here?"

Finally, the judge can no longer pretend he does not hear any of this and booms, "Counselor, I believe your client is up here."

The little man spins as though hit by a bullet, waves his hand in the air, and strides to the bench.

"Thank you, Your Honor. May I have a moment with my client?"

"A moment."

Lawyer and client disappear into a corner. Count to two. Enter, lawyer and client.

"If I may proceed, Your Honor."

"Go ahead." Jones steps up to the witness stand and is sworn.

His learned counselor: "Mr. Jones, we are here today to ask this honorable court to restore unlimited driving privileges to you. Do you recall why those privileges were taken from you?"

"Yessir. Drunk driving."

"And what limitations were placed upon your privileges?"

"I can drive home to work. Work to home."

"And have you honored those limitations?"

"Huh?" Suddenly everyone in the room is listening.

"Well, sir, do you drive directly from home to work?"

"Yeah."

"And directly from work to home?"

"Yeah. Directly. . . . Unless I stop along the way or somethin'."

Now even the judge is listening.

"Uh, Mr. Jones, let me ask you this. When did you last have a drink?"

"Well, let's see. This is *Wednesday*, right?"

The lawyer quickly shifts to another approach.

"Eh, Mr. Jones, you don't drink and then drive around town or anything, correct?"

"No, sir. If I have a drink or two, I drive straight back to my house."

At this, it seems as if all the people in the room simultaneously turn to look at the person sitting next to them. Everyone, that is, except the judge, who has no one next to him and so jerks his head in first one direction and then the other, as if watching a heated tennis match. Throats are cleared and a few snickers surface.

I have never known what it meant to "gird your loins" until then, but I behold Jones's lawyer girding as best he can. Finally, after a pause lasting too long, he speaks.

"Mr. Jones, let me put it to you directly: Since your privileges were restricted, have you engaged in any drunk driving?"

"No."

"Thank you."

"I mean, it takes a *lot* for me to get drunk and—"

"Thank you, Mr. Jones!" The lawyer walks back to counsel table and ungirds.

The judge looks at the state's lawyer, whose mouth hangs open. He just blinks at the judge and shrugs. "Nothing?" the judge asks.

"No questions," the state's lawyer replies.

Jones smiles at the state's lawyer and says, "Hey, thanks." He then rises from the witness box, walks to his lawyer, and whispers a few words to him.

"Well . . ." the judge begins, ready to rule. But Jones's lawyer interrupts.

"If I may, Your Honor, my client informs me that he has brought a character witness."

"You're not serious."

"Your Honor, please . . ."

"Okay. But briefly."

From the back of the room emerges a grizzled, potbellied, T-shirted man in his sixties who could not have looked more grim if he were attending his own wake. He shuffles to the stand, drops into the seat, swears to tell the truth, and starts rocking back and forth. Something—maybe the chair, maybe the man himself—is creaking.

"Sir, would you state your name for the record, please?"

"Yeah."

Another one of those long pauses.

"Your name, please!"

"What? Oh. Smith. Ed Smith."

"Mr. Smith, do you know Mr. Jones?"

"Kind of."

"Well, how do you know him?"

"Neighbors."

"Have you had occasion to talk with Mr. Jones and get to know him?"

"Sure. Why not."

"And what is your impression of his character?"

"He's okay. I got no complaints."

The lawyer puffs up his chest. He takes on the fire of a man with nothing left to lose. "Well, sir, you were aware of the fact that his driving privileges were limited?"

"Sure."

"And you knew this was inconvenient for him?"

"Sure."

"And embarrassing?"

"Sure."

"And is it your impression he has learned his lesson?"

"Yeah. I think so. Why not."

"And based on your knowledge of my client's character, is it your opin-ion that he would ever drive while drunk again?"

The state's lawyer apparently senses that, while the winds in his favor are not shifting, they are at least stalling out a bit. He rises to object, but then pauses when he notes that Smith has also paused. He sits back down.

"Well, I guess I don't know. But I'll tell you this: If he goes back to driving like he used to, with all that drinking and all, *he's gonna kill some-body someday.*"

At these last words Smith stabs the air with his finger for emphasis. He sits back with a creak, satisfied. And then he looks over at Jones and gives him a big smile that says, There, son, I sure hope that helped. And, bizarrely, Jones gives him back a smile that says, It sure did. Thanks for everything.

I was so stunned that I did not even hear what happened next. I did not hear whether the judge ordered an execution, or demanded a flogging, or entered an injunction forbidding Jones from ever again operating any-thing that had a moving part.

Now whenever I tell this story people think I'm making it up. And one of my greatest professional regrets is that I did not hurdle over the railing that day and immediately order a transcript. But I can assure you that something very much like this really happened.

I remember it well.

And I remember it better every time I tell it.

LEONARD M. NIEHOFF
BUTZEL LONG
ANN ARBOR, MICHIGAN

What's in a Word?

Early in my career, shortly after I finished my clerkship to the judge who presided over the pornography trial involving the embarrassed pig, I received an appointment as an assistant United States attorney. Assistant United States attorneys are the lawyers who represent the government in court. They are generally young lawyers, and while some handle civil cases, most prosecute criminal cases. My first trial involved the prosecution of a defendant charged with assaulting a federal law enforcement officer . . .to be more precise, an investigator with the Immigration Service. The chief witness was the defendant's brother.

I hadn't originated this prosecution. Some other more senior prosecutor in our office had done that. He asked me if I wanted to get some experience trying a case he had on his docket. I was brand-new to the office and eager to learn. So I said, Sure, that'd be great. What I didn't do was ask to see the file first. You see, this other prosecutor had a reason for trying to unload this case. I didn't learn it until trial.

The defendant was a Greek laborer who had been naturalized as a U.S. citizen after a quickly arranged marriage to an American woman. It seems that the Greek community in my town had developed a network in which young Greek men were assisted in entering the country illegally and then given the benefit of arranged marriages to young American women who received both a fee and a strong, hardworking husband for their efforts. In our country, lawful permanent residence comes with marriage to an American.

The defendant's brother (not yet married, and awaiting his arranged bride) had been hiding in the defendant's basement, ever since he entered the United States illegally a week or so before. He spoke no English and apparently did not understand that he shouldn't open the door to anyone. After responding to the knock and seeing two burly dark-suited men standing before him, he quickly ran into the basement. When the defendant arrived downstairs, he saw his brother, frightened out of his wits, holding for dear life onto a support pole while the two Immigration officers were trying to pry him loose and arrest him. The defendant, seeing that the jig was up, placed his arm on the closer of the Immigration officers and explained that his brother spoke no English and was simply afraid.

"Please," he said, in his best broken English, "to let go my brother. I tell him who you are and that he must go with you."

The Immigration officers let go of the brother. After the defendant explained the situation to his brother, he released his grip on the support pole and allowed himself to be taken away. Weeks later the defendant was charged with assault, for nothing more than the hand he had placed on the Immigration officer's arm so that he could explain that his frightened and confused brother spoke no English. It wasn't the best of cases for the prosecution.

What I'll never forget is my cross-examination of the brother, the one who couldn't speak English. The court had provided a translator who stood next to the witness box and repeated my questions to the witness in Greek, and then repeated his answers, given in Greek, into translated English to judge, jury, counsel—and the spectator gallery that was completely filled with members of the Greek community. I remember that the brother kept smiling at me during the entire cross-examination as though he was sincerely polite to me, a government man, a man of authority.

I established through my examination that the witness had indeed entered the country illegally, that he had been hiding in his brother's house awaiting his wedding day to the woman who had been arranged for him, and that when the two burly Americans in dark suits chased him into the basement he was indeed frightened. You see, I learned through the translator, in the witness's country, government men like that might well be there to kill you. Then, finally, we turned to assault. (The other brother's hand on the arm of one of the officers, telling him, "Please to let go my brother.") That is where I can safely say the defendant's fate was decided. Remember, now, all this is being done through a translator.

ME: So, Mr. [witness], do you understand that your brother is accused of having done something serious?

WITNESS [after translation]: No.

ME [showing the jury my disbelief that the witness could answer the question in the negative. Remember, I'm a young and

inexperienced lawyer here, playing this a bit overdramatically]:
Are you telling this honorable court, and this jury of your
brother's peers that you do not understand the charges placed
against your brother? These most serious of charges? Is that
your testimony? [I might even have pointed an accusatory finger
at the witness. I think I did.]

WITNESS [after translation]: Huh?

ME [showing my exasperation for the benefit of the jury]: Well then,
let me ask you this. Do you understand what assault is?

WITNESS [after translation]: Sure.

ME [now facing the jury, my back to the witness, because my next
question will be the coup de grâce, the only one that Perry
Mason would ask, bringing the witness forward in his seat, lips
quivering, hysterical. This was going to be it.]: Well, then, sir,
why don't you just tell this jury what assault is?

WITNESS [I see the translator listen to the witness, then he looks at
me, but he remains silent. He seems not to want to repeat the
answer. So, sternly, I demand of the translator, "The witness's
answer please!" The translator looks at me a moment longer,
then he shrugs and repeats the witness's answer]: You got a salt,
and then you got a pepper. They both usually on the table in two
little shakers.

I'll admit it took a little longer for the jury to stop laughing than I
would have preferred. I remember looking up to the judge for some assistance here. But he seemed to be laughing so hard I thought it best simply
to wait for the entire courtroom to calm down.

It did, eventually. Those who remember this case will tell you that the
jury's deliberation might have been the shortest in the history of the court.
But I think that might be an overstatement. There must have been some
other, shorter, not-guilty verdict.

The spectator gallery, the defendant, and his brother (the translator
rendering assistance) all invited me as an honored guest to the celebration
party they had quickly planned at a local Greek restaurant.

As the prosecutor, I thought it prudent not to attend. Later, I learned
that there had been several toasts in my honor.

I wasn't sure how to take that.

R.L.

Disorder in the Court III

QUESTION: Did you stop along the way?

ANSWER: Several times. We stopped several times because of the little boy. And we ate at least twice that I know of, and we got gas.

QUESTION: Now, Officer, besides the flushed face, the weaving motion, the staggering gait, and the odor of alcohol emitting from his breath, did you notice anything else unusual about the defendant before you arrested him?

ANSWER: Yes. His speech was slick and third—or sick and furled—or, I mean, he was very incoherent.

QUESTION: I understand.

QUESTION: Earlier in the deposition you said you lost the tip of a finger in a blender accident, is that correct?

ANSWER: Uh-huh, yes.

QUESTION: May I ask which finger?

ANSWER: (indicating)

QUESTION: You thoroughly enjoyed that, didn't you, ma'am?

Stuck-Up

I REPRESENTED AN ELDERLY MAN IN A PATERNITY CASE. HE WAS keeping company with a rather rotund woman. In order for her to continue to receive her government aid, the local social services required her to identify the father of her child and seek child support from him. She asked. He refused. So she sued him.

After receiving the paternity complaint and the claim for child support, my client contacted me. When we met to discuss the case, he was adamant that while she and he did have sex—apparently repeatedly and regularly—he was sure that she was using a contraceptive. He described the pill and assured me that he had observed her taking the pill daily. He insisted on a trial because he knew that he could not be the father.

The day of the trial came and the parties appeared before the court. The state's first witness was the woman. She testified that she and my client had sex at approximately the time the child was conceived. On cross-examination she admitted that she had been using a contraceptive pill and that she took it religiously.

"And you take the pill every day?"

"Yes, sir."

I then asked the next question, fully expecting the obvious answer.

"How exactly do you take the pill?"

Her reply was not so expected.

"I stuck it up me like I always do."

Needless to say the courtroom erupted in laughter. The judge had to turn away and her lawyer was doubled over. After order was restored my client said loudly enough for everyone to hear, "See? I told you she was taking the pill!"

LAW OFFICES
CHARLES D. DECKER
DOTHAN, ALABAMA

The Oath

THE WITNESS HAD FINISHED HIS FINAL STATEMENT BY SAYING with great passion, "So help me, if that isn't the truth, may God strike me down!"

Just then a large ornately carved cornice from our aging courthouse broke from the ceiling and smashed to the floor directly behind the witness.

In the stunned silence that followed, the judge dismissed the witness, who hurriedly left the courtroom several shades paler than when he arrived.

DIRK LARSEN
LARSEN LAW FIRM PLLC
GREAT FALLS, MONTANA

Consumed with Evidence

I WAS A DEFENSE ATTORNEY IN A MEDICAL MALPRACTICE CASE brought by a woman who had developed ovarian cancer. She claimed that her doctor had failed to diagnose her tumor when it was small and manageable, and still treatable. Instead, the tumor had grown. To prove his point to the jury, the plaintiff's attorney produced an orange, which he claimed was the size of her actual tumor. He offered the orange into evidence as Exhibit C.

After the lunch break we reconvened in the courtroom to resume the trial. One of the other defense attorneys stood to cross-examine the witness. As he approached the witness he asked the clerk for Exhibit C. The clerk rushed around trying to find Exhibit C. After a few minutes one of the jurors raised his hand and sheepishly admitted that he had eaten Exhibit C during the lunch break.

KATHERINE M. HANNA
SHEEHAN PHINNEY BASS + GREEN
MANCHESTER, NEW HAMPSHIRE

Fender Benders

I'M A PERSONAL INJURY LAWYER. THERE ARE TIMES WHEN MY practice is as much entertainment as it is lawyering. Here are two deposition transcript excerpts that show you why. I've changed the names of the parties and condensed the testimony. Otherwise, they're exactly as they happened.

I Can See Clearly Now

On June 2, 1994, Mr. Jackson was operating his boss's 1986 Cadillac on Pennsylvania Street in Indianapolis. As Mr. Jackson was approaching the intersection of Pennsylvania Street and the I-70 off-ramp, a car operated by Mr. Smith ignored a red traffic control signal. The ensuing collision demolished both vehicles and sent Mr. Jackson to the hospital with a left hip fracture. Mr. Smith was not injured and claimed that the light controlling his lane of travel was in fact green, rather than red, and that my client, Mr. Jackson, was at fault for the collision.

Mr. Smith was questioned at his deposition:

Q. How long have you had a driver's license?
A. Fifteen years.
Q. Do you have any restrictions on your driver's license?
A. No.
Q. Are you sure that you did not have any restrictions to drive a motor vehicle at the time of the collision?
A. Yes.
Q. Sir, your driver's record indicates that you must wear glasses while operating a motor vehicle.
A. That's true.

Q. I am confused. Is it your testimony now that you were required to wear glasses while operating a motor vehicle?

A. Well, yes, of course.

Q. Who is your eye doctor?

A. I do not have one.

Q. Who prescribed or filled your eyeglass prescription?

A. I don't know.

Q. How long have you had your glasses?

A. I am not sure. You would have to ask my brother.

Q. What does your brother have to do with your eyeglasses?

A. These are my brother's eyeglasses. When he got a new pair, he gave me his old ones.

Q. Were you wearing glasses at the time of the collision?

A. No.

Q. How was your vision, without glasses, at the time of the collision?

A. I couldn't see a thing.

Just Asking

A homeless man was a passenger in a vehicle operated by his friend. A teenager attempted to turn left and struck the vehicle in which the homeless man was a passenger. The homeless man was taken to the emergency room with multiple fractures and was in the hospital for about a month. After he was discharged, the homeless man sought legal counsel.

At the initial client meeting, the man's legal remedies were discussed. The homeless man stated that the fractures were not as bad as his inability to achieve an erection. Consequently, the man was treated by a urologist for his sexual dysfunction.

At his deposition, the homeless man testified:

Q. What other problems do you have now?

A. I can't get it up.

Q. Do you mean you are unable to achieve and maintain an erection?

A. Yes, unless I get a shot.

Q.   What kind of shot?

A.   I have a needle with some medicine that I inject directly into my thing.

Q.   Your thing?

A.   My dick.

Q.   Okay.

A.   Damn thing hurts so bad.

Q.   I understand.

A.   Worst thing is that I get a woodie that lasts forever.

Q.   Is that bad?

A.   Yeah, it's bad. My woodie lasts upwards of four hours. I can't pee or put my pants on. It just ain't worth it.

Q.   What is the name of that medicine, by the way?

DANIEL S. CHAMBERLAIN
CONOUR • DOEHRMAN
ATTORNEYS AT LAW
INDIANAPOLIS, INDIANA

Combat

THE JUSTICE SYSTEM OFTEN PATS ITSELF ON THE BACK BY TOUT-
ing the "adversarial system"—said to be a great "engine of truth." Maybe.
But most trial lawyers will tell you that a courtroom scene resembles combat—and if the truth should raise its head over the bunker, that is more
coincidence than design.

In the course of the fight between plaintiff (or prosecutor) and the defendant, the defense attorney scrambles to control the plan of battle—
keeping an eye on the jury, another on the judge, another on his opponent,
yet another on his script and notes, and trying to heed the tugs on his arm
from a client who may have nothing more to contribute than "The S.O.B.
[the witness on the stand] is lying!" Tension—thy name is "trial proceedings."

My client was charged with the crime of criminal sexual conduct
("CSC"), which is a legal euphemism concocted by the legislature to ex-
haust the variations on what was once the old, simple rape statute. Thus,
we now have criminal sexual conduct, first-degree, or second-degree, or
third-degree, or fourth-degree—to reflect the relative standing of sinful-
ness and evil, it would appear.

The offense allegedly committed by my client was that of sexually mo-
lesting his fifteen-year-old stepdaughter. According to the stepdaughter,
he had come upon her late one evening and attempted to do awful things
to her. The facts developed seemed to indicate that no sexual penetration
had occurred, so my client was not likely to be convicted of CSC-1 (an offense punishable by life in prison). CSC-2 (which involves what used to be
known as "heavy petting") was still a real possibility—and the penalty was
fifteen years in prison.

As any criminal lawyer will tell you, these cases are hardly fun to try.
There is an understandable and natural tendency for the jurors to take at
face value any testimony from a child—more so here where the child was

female and of a vulnerable age. My client, on the other hand, while only about thirty, did not have what we lawyers call jury appeal. He was horrible-looking, pale and withdrawn; he reminded me of a funeral director. Nothing could persuade him to lighten up and present a different countenance to the jury. Relentlessly, the trial wore on. And it didn't look good for my client.

My last tactical choice was to bear down on the victim. Not a happy choice, because jurors are known to resent lawyers who seem to pick on a child witness. Nonetheless, I was able to get the alleged victim to narrow her tale of woe to a single incident, which took place on one of three Friday nights in June. She was certain of this because she knew it had happened "after school was out in June" and before "she went to her aunt's" in a distant town on July 4. The exact time was further established as "right after I watched *The Dukes of Hazzard*," a TV show airing at about 10:00 P.M. each Friday.

My client provided me with his "logs." He was a trucker by trade and by law was required to keep a log of his time and travel. This is pretty reliable and trustworthy evidence, and his log showed him to be miles and miles away on the first of the three possible Friday nights in June. No crime on the first available Friday.

Some hurried investigation on my part established that the TV program did not play on the second Friday in question—it had been preempted by a baseball game. Not to be outdone, the prosecutor showed that *The Dukes of Hazzard* did appear, albeit on other channels available on cable. And my client had cable service.

Call it dumb luck, fortuity, adversarial accident, or whatever. A quick telephone call to the TV cable provider established that my client had failed to pay his cable bill the preceding month, so that his cable service was suspended. Cut off. No cable service on that second Friday that the crime might have occurred.

One more Friday to disprove in order to shatter the girl's claim and thus sow doubt in the minds of the jury. I had almost given up. I prolonged the testimony a bit more, and then I inquired of the young lady why she had taken so long to inform anyone of this occurrence. Our information had been that she had complained only after she arrived at her aunt's, after July 4.

"Oh," she responded, "I told some friends about it a week before I went to my aunt's."

Bingo! Then it obviously could not have taken place on the Friday immediately prior to July 4. That had been the third and last possible Friday.

Needless to say, the case then concluded, and the jury heard me argue the factual impossibility of the commission of the crime on any of the three Fridays. They retired to deliberate, after the prosecutor's final words and the judge's final instructions.

It is here where one should realize the tension that has built up in the defense attorney, who has had to carefully orchestrate every move, every argument, every objection, every nuance. Then comes the end, and he must then orate with eloquence—summing up and trying to persuade the jury of his client's innocence, or at least that the case against his client has not been proved beyond a reasonable doubt. And then the jury files out to deliberate. And then the lawyer begins the gnawing examination of his conscience. Did I do everything I should have? Did I fail my client in any way? It is a terrible time of soul-searching.

At last the "buzzer" sounds—the jury has reached a verdict. The tension mounts once more. The adrenaline flows. Stand. Face the jury, as they file in.

Slowly the judge protracts the agony by his routine inquiries. Have you reached a verdict? The foreman assents. The moments of waiting seem endless until the jury foreman at last utters the fateful words. *Not guilty.*

Thank God. The bubble bursts. At last the tension is relieved. And then comes the sweet afterglow as the defense attorney basks in the attention and the congratulations, knowing now that he has successfully performed the legal miracle expected. The client smiles—at last. The jurors smile benignly. The relatives and friends in the first row smile. All's well with the world. Victory. Truth has prevailed.

Or has it? Has justice been done—or has the prosecutor simply failed to convince the jury? The case was "not proven." But that is our system. We all are presumed innocent until proven guilty. But did a truly guilty man get off? And did I do this? Is this really a triumph of the adversarial system? But the combat is over. Time for the troops to leave the battlefield.

Tomorrow there will be another war.

MILTON J. MAROVICH
ATTORNEY AT LAW
KALAMAZOO, MICHIGAN

Stiffed

THE DEFENDANT WAS A DOCTOR. THOUGH HE HAD A FAMILY practice in Macon, Georgia, he was born, raised, and trained in a foreign country. He was under indictment for numerous sex crimes with his female patients. We sued him in the civil courts on behalf of another of his patients, this one a man who had claimed that the doctor had improperly prescribed the drug Desyrel. Unfortunately, the drug the doctor administered to our client caused him to contract a medical condition known as priapism. This condition causes prolonged, painful erections. If left untreated, priapism results in impotency, blood clots, and gangrene.

During the deposition, I asked the doctor what he told my client when he realized that he had contracted a very serious medical condition. He responded as follows in a heavy Spanish accent;

"I say to him, 'Oh, no! No, no! We have killed Mr. Peter.'"

We settled the case shortly thereafter.

TRACEY L. DELLACONA, R.N., J.D.
ATTORNEY AT LAW
MACON, GEORGIA

Can You Hear Me?

DURING MY FIRST YEAR OF LAW PRACTICE, THE SENIOR PARTNER of our firm let me work on the case of John Burney, a man who suddenly disappeared from a rural Arkansas town. He was insured by our client, a well-known insurance company, to the tune of $1 million. Months went by without a trace of him. If he were proven dead, his wife stood to become rich on our clients' money. All evidence pointed to Burney's death, with the exception of a single witness who, it appeared, had seen him alive: a deaf-mute named Nat.

I reported to the senior partner that Nat was the key to everything. Deposition testimony was needed. My boss asked me to find an interpreter. I did. A week later the lawyers, the presumed widow, Nat, and the interpreter all appeared for Nat's deposition.

Nat and the interpreter were both sworn to tell the truth. Since the deposition was being held in the local courthouse of the rather small town from which Burney had disappeared, a crowd had gathered. With the stage fully set, the court reporter ready to tap away, and counsel for Mrs. Burney ready to cross-examine as needed, my senior partner asked the interpreter to inquire whether Nat knew the disappeared man.

The interpreter solemnly took in the question, turned to face Nat, and screamed at the top of his lungs, "DO YOU KNOW JOHN BURNEY?"

Poor Nat grunted a forty-five-second answer unintelligible in any language. Seemingly unfazed by this interpretive method, my senior partner spoke.

SENIOR PARTNER: "What did the witness just say?"
INTERPRETER: "I have absolutely no idea."

After a few more screaming questions from the interpreter, followed by answers he could not interpret, a woman spoke up from the back of the courtroom. She told us that in response to the first question with the forty-five-second answer, Nat had said yes.

My senior partner invited the woman up to the deposition table and asked how she knew Nat's answer. She responded that she was Nat's common-law wife and had no difficulty understanding him. The woman was promptly sworn in and became our new interpreter.

Now my senior partner questioned the woman, who in turn questioned Nat. Her questions were a combination of wild hand gestures, grunts, and caveman-like English. A series of questions designed to learn whether Nat knew the disappearing John Burney, had seen him the night of his disappearance, and possibly knew his whereabouts resulted in a variety of answers from Nat. Some were short, some quite long, but all sounded the same. In response to one question, Nat grunted a quick series of short random syllables. When the woman was asked to interpret, she gave an elaborate answer lasting a full minute to the effect that Nat had seen John Burney on the night of his disappearance as he walked away into the Mississippi Delta carrying a large brown bag full of money. Conversely, when Nat would garble a long and elaborate string of guttural sounds, the woman would simply say that his answer was yes.

After tolerating as much of this as he could, the lawyer for the hopeful widow broke in sharply:

"I object! This witness answers for up to a minute, then the interpreter tells us he said yes. Yet when the witness gives a one- or two-syllable response, the interpreter gives us a lengthy account lasting nearly a minute. I strenuously object."

Our new interpreter sighed and actually rolled her eyes. Without prompting, she announced that she was able to effectively interpret—and to do so accurately—because Nat had told her the story of the disappearing man many, many times before.

Needless to say, we lost the case. John Burney was eventually presumed dead, and the insurance money was paid to the very grateful widow.

John Burney later surfaced under an assumed name in Key West, Florida, remarried and with a new family.

JAMES M. SIMPSON
FRIDAY, ELDREDGE & CLARK
LITTLE ROCK, ARKANSAS

An Evil Genius

I RECEIVED A CALL FROM A SMALL-TIME CRIMINAL CLIENT named Fisk, who lived in a town just outside London. He complained of being constantly harassed by local police. Fisk was apparently unmoved by my suggestion that a proper job, on the straight and narrow, might go a long way toward solving his problem. After giving my suggestion the scant attention he evidently felt it deserved, he hit upon a clever idea. To outwit the police, he would change his name.

"To what?" I asked.

The new name he would take, the fellow informed me, was "Fisk."

"How exactly would that throw the police off the scent?" I asked. "Since not only is Fisk your name now, but you will be living in the same house, driving the same car, etc. . . ."

"Ah, but don't you see," he replied, with an obvious tone of impatience reserved for those dimmer bulbs like myself, not clever enough to keep up, "I'm changing it to Fisc—with a *c*."

DAVID WALSH
SIMONS MUIRHEAD & BURTON
LONDON, ENGLAND

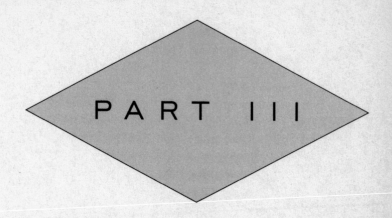

PART III

ALL RISE FOR THE JUDGE

I'VE ALWAYS CONSIDERED A JUDGE TO BE A COMBINATION AIR traffic controller and absolute ruler of a small kingdom called the courtroom. The judge has to control the process by which disputes, both great and small, are resolved. He or she also has to rule the place, maintaining both order and a deep respect for the law to work its magic.

Most, if not all, judges are lawyers. And most have had earlier careers as litigators, regularly appearing before other judges. So they have seen it all from both sides. How they put up, day in and day out, with some of the goings-on before them is truly a wonder. I do believe that the most successful judges mix their intellect with a strong dash of humorous appreciation for the human condition.

The following stories depict some of what can, and does, happen while the judge is presiding, trying to ensure that justice is done.

The Appearance of Evil

THE DEFENDANTS ON TRIAL IN FRONT OF THE LATE JUDGE IRV-
ing Ben Cooper in New York were charged with violating the Mann Act,
which prohibits the interstate transportation of women for prostitution.
The defendants were the pimps. The prosecution's witnesses were the call
girls themselves and their madams. With all these characters the courtroom looked like the judicial version of *Guys and Dolls*.

The defense lawyer—let's call him Mr. Slick—wanted to exclude the
government's witnesses from sitting in the courtroom during the trial. He
didn't want the ladies of the night to hear one another's testimony, in the
legitimate concern that they might tailor their stories to fit together. He
needed to point out inconsistencies on cross-examination to create reasonable doubt in the minds of the jury. So he made the standard motion
to exclude all witnesses. The judge granted the motion and ordered the
young ladies and their "chaperones" to wait outside the courtroom until
each was called to the witness stand.

Sometime during the first witnesses' testimony the eager young prosecutor—let's call him Mr. Doright—noticed a statuesque and voluptuous
blond among the spectators. She was wearing clinging leopard pants and
a revealing blouse under a silver mink boa. Her neck was adorned by a ser-
pentine necklace in glittering gold. Her eyes were shaded a provocative
blue, and her long false eyelashes were as obvious as her long red fingernails.

She appeared to be intent on the proceedings and she smiled coyly in
the direction of the defense table.

Ever on the alert, Mr. Doright rose and asked to approach the bench
in order to speak to the judge out of the hearing of the jury. Judge Cooper
told him and Mr. Slick to approach.

"There is a woman in the courtroom," Mr. Doright said, "and I am
mindful of Your Honor's order excluding witnesses, who appears to be a

lady of easy virtue, and I wonder whether Your Honor might inquire into whether she plans to testify as a defense witness."

"Really?" said Judge Cooper in his most judicious manner. "Where is she seated?"

"She's the blonde in the first row," the young prosecutor informed the court.

"Your Honor!" said Mr. Slick. "That's my wife!"

"Proceed," said the judge without even cracking a smile, as the embarrassed Mr. Doright remembered that one of the first things he had been taught in law school was never jump to conclusions.

JAMES D. ZIRIN
BROWN & WOOD LLP
NEW YORK, NEW YORK

Principles of Lawyering

THERE ARE CERTAIN PRINCIPLES OF LAWYERING ONE SHOULD never forget. One of the first principles I learned many years ago: There are many cases you cannot win; there is no case you cannot lose.

My son Cameron needed someone to rectify a clerical error—wrong middle name—on his birth certificate. Not my legal specialty, but as happens in our profession, I got the call—from my wife. Well, okay, so how difficult could this be for me, a litigator of complex cases? With hardly a second thought (as will become fairly apparent), I took charge. I suggested to my wife that she fill in the necessary forms. No problem. The petition is finalized, the proposed judge's order is prepared. I sign on the dotted line. A quick appearance before a judge and *voilà, c'est fini.* This is how things should work in life, I'm thinking, particularly mine.

Into the judge's chambers we march at 9:00 in the morning; I the lawyer, my wife, and the petitioner, Cameron. Now the family can see what a real lawyer does, unlike that silly TV stuff. I greet the judge, introduce the players, hand over the paperwork, and confidently await the payoff. I should have had an inkling of what lay ahead when His Honor began poring over the petition as if it were the will of a family member. Without warning, it began.

"Can you waive publication, Counselor?" the judge asks, his eyes still buried in the petition.

The thought of waving goodbye had crossed my mind. I didn't think that's what he said. Fortunately, as a trial lawyer, I'm used to thinking on my feet. Without hesitation I reply.

"Say what, Your Honor?"

"I see your petition waives publication. Can you do that?" the judge inquires, still studying the document.

He's kidding, isn't he? We certainly could, as far as I was concerned. We could waive this whole proceeding, in fact. Being a lawyer of some experience, however, my instincts tell me to hold my tongue. The judge seems to think that this is the problem.

"Well, Counselor, are you going to answer my question?" the judge asks, his eyes still pinned to the petition.

His reasons for threatening the congenial atmosphere of this early-morning get-together are totally beyond me, but I let it pass. (Judges have tough jobs and are sometimes irritable. Be patient with them and there is a 40 percent chance they will be patient with you—a major principle that experienced trial lawyers know.)

"Judge, in my opinion, publication can be waived," I assert, in my best Solomon-like tones, the same as if I had a considered opinion. (That should put him at ease. Judges handle a lot of matters and they can't be experts at everything. It's my job to help out when I can and I'm happy to do it.)

"In my opinion, publication can be waived," the judge replies.

Exactly. I was sure I said it first, but I am willing to let him take the credit if it will make a difference. (If a judge is agreeing with you, no sense in arguing about who crossed the plate first. A minor, yet important rule.)

"In my opinion, publication can be waived," the judge says again.

Don't get me wrong, I like judges who hang on my every word, but it did occur to me he was overdoing it a bit. Very slowly, I begin to retrace in my mind exactly how I had come to be here, in this place, at this time, before this person, on this mission.

"I assume you're relying on Title 19, Section 23.3, Counselor?" he asks.

No reason to get personal here, I think. And then suddenly it strikes me. Hey, wait a minute . . . just one darn minute, please. Now, he wants to know if I've read *the law.* Does this man not know I am a former law professor? Has he forgotten that I successfully prosecuted major felonies in federal court? Can he be unaware that I personally have the autograph of Justice Potter Stewart?

Well, okay, so I hadn't actually *read* the law. This is a petition for a change of a middle name and no one objects, for God's sake. Perhaps I have not made myself clear; he thinks this is a major criminal conspiracy and I have just applied for a warrant to search the governor's mansion. Fortunately, I didn't actually say any of these things. (One does not share every thought with His Honor when it is not absolutely necessary. As principles go, this is for sure in the top ten.)

"That citation sounds right to me, Judge," I say, figuring he will be impressed by my recall matching his.

"Sounds right to me, Judge," he says, once again seriously failing to make eye contact. Worse, he appears to be talking to himself again. "Sounds right to me, Judge," he repeats to no one in particular. The man is clearly out of control, I'm thinking. I notice Cameron looking around the office for the source of this echo chamber. My wife makes a quick assessment of the developing situation and quietly slips on her sunglasses.

"Some lawyers think Superior Court judges have the power to do anything, regardless of what the law is," the judge says.

There's no denying the man is on a roll.

"However, those lawyers are sadly mistaken."

I was just beginning to feel some sympathy for those sadly mistaken lawyers when he looks up from the paperwork. At long last, I thought, he realizes that fooling with me will do him no good.

Put another way, he had concluded this hearing was over. (A significant principle to remember is that judges are very time conscious.)

"It can't be done," he says, as he hands back the petition. "Good to see you folks; drop by anytime."

Oh, sure thing, Your Honor. Once every millennium ought to be sufficient. Cameron leads the way out, thinking this was not at all like *LA Law*. A lady with sunglasses clutching a scarf over her head falls in behind him, single file. I try to keep pace, but crawling on all fours hampers my speed.

As I was saying, there are many cases you cannot win. For his part, Cameron still has the wrong middle name, and I am in the library researching the legal meaning of *publication*.

In reflecting on this matter, there is a corollary to the "first principle" noted above. It's one I used to recite to my school-age children: "I know what you want is important, but do your homework first, then we'll talk." Something tells me the judge would have liked that. I can just see him saying it to himself . . . once, twice, maybe even three times.

C. Michael Abbott
Attorney at Law
Atlanta, Georgia

The Wisdom of the Court

THE FOLLOWING STORY WAS TOLD TO ME BY A JUDGE WHO swore it was true.

Before he became a judge, Raulston Schoolfield was representing a woman who, along with her husband, had been charged with keeping a house of ill repute. At trial the jury convicted both Judge Schoolfield's client and her husband, who was represented by another lawyer. The case was promptly appealed.

Schoolfield's legal point on appeal was that since a woman in Tennessee was required by law to reside with her husband, then it could only be the husband who was guilty of operating the house. The wife had no choice but to live there. Anyway, that was the legal argument.

At the appeal the chief justice of the State Supreme Court, Alexander Chambliss, inquired as to whether or not the court could deduce that, typically, the type of establishment in question was operated by a woman.

Without thinking, Schoolfield replied, "Your Honor, I am not experienced in these matters, but if Your Honor is then I bow to the wisdom of the court."

Conviction affirmed.

DAVID P. HAWLEY
ATTORNEY AT LAW
CHATTANOOGA, TENNESSEE

Justice Skirted

DURING THE DAYS WHEN MINISKIRTS WERE POPULAR FOR the first time, I represented a very pretty, well-built young woman who had a "no contest" divorce pending. She and her husband had simply decided to call it quits. There were no assets, no property rights, no alimony, and no children involved. We had all the pleadings in place and had scheduled a fifteen-minute hearing before the court to finalize the process.

I was standing in the courtroom with my client, who was dressed in a quite abbreviated skirt, showing a lot of long leg, when the judge entered and began his ascent to the bench. Now, this particular judge was one of the most senior members of the court. He had a reputation as a fair-minded, no-nonsense jurist, but was a bit on the old-fashioned side. I saw him take a step or two up toward the bench, glance absently in our direction, pause, glance again, then retrace his steps down to the floor level and look out at my client, giving her the "up and down."

The judge asked very audibly, "Counsel, is that your client?"

"Yes, Your Honor," I dutifully responded.

The judge looked once again at my client. Then, as he turned on his heel, he said, "You take her home, put some clothes on her, and come back another day." And with that he left the courtroom, with my client's mouth agape and me speechless. Not daunted, and clearly furious at the judge's remark, my client left my side and headed for the door to the judge's chambers, shouting, "Hey, hey."

The bailiff quickly restrained her, told her she better do what the judge said, and we left, only to have her berate me, the system, judges, and life in general.

Well, short skirts are once again in fashion. Once I determine that my female client's case has been assigned to this particular senior judge, I suggest she dress in the style favored by Whistler's mother.

I tell them it's either that or justice will be skirted.

DAVID F. KERN
ATTORNEY AT LAW
PALM HARBOR, FLORIDA

The Dream Merchant

LONG BEFORE I WAS APPOINTED TO THE BENCH, EARLY IN MY legal career, I was a prosecutor. That was when I first met Guido Franch. I don't believe I've met anyone like him since.

Franch had a third-grade education and had spent time as a coalminer. But he had a talent. Franch knew how to separate people from their money. He did it with a small packet of green powder. With it, Franch claimed that he could turn ordinary tap water into high-octane gasoline. And people believed him: simple people, sophisticated people, poor people, and wealthy people. Here's what happened.

Franch claimed that he had no idea how or why the formula that made up the green powder worked. He received the formula, he said, from a German refugee, a mining engineer whom Franch had befriended during his coalmining days. He would always refer to the engineer as "the Doctor." The Doctor was old and in ill health, in fact he was dying—or so Franch's story went. On his deathbed, the Doctor entrusted the formula to his friend Franch, extracting from him the solemn promise that he would always seek to use the formula for the benefit of mankind, ensuring that it would never fall into the wrong hands. At this point in his story, Franch would explain that the wrong hands meant the big oil companies, who would seek to use the formula for greed and avarice, and not for good.

The formula the Doctor entrusted to Franch was something he had developed out of his experiments with coal. He had somehow managed to extract the chemical secret of energy from these experiments. At this point, Franch would say that he had no idea how or why the formula worked. But it did. And then he would provide a little demonstration using some green powder and any supply of water his prospective investor had at hand. And from a modest investment, Franch would claim, untold wealth would flow like the high-octane liquid this green powdered miracle of science had just produced. And, as I said, people invested.

One of his investors was a wealthy Texan named Charles T. Coleman. Coleman got the pitch, then the demonstration. Then he was hooked. He put up some money for the formula; more was to follow after some laboratory testing. He received what Franch claimed was one half of the formula, the rest to follow after testing—and, of course, more money. Once he got the money, Franch became scarce. After more than too many requests for the rest of the formula with nothing but empty promises from Franch, Coleman came to us. After an investigation, we prosecuted.

In preparing for trial I compiled a list of people who had given Franch money. In fact, after the charges were brought, a whole series of Franch's investors showed up, complaining bitterly about the arrest. All of them had witnessed Franch make gas out of water. Rainwater, tap water, creek water. It made no difference, these people claimed. One after another, they told me, add the green "stuff" and the result was gasoline.

At trial I called a whole series of witnesses, all of whom had given money to Franch. Blue-collar workers, young mothers, widows—even a priest who had advanced money from his own pocket "to help the poor of the parish." Each witness related the same story: the green powder, the story of the dying Doctor, the demonstration. On cross-examination, Franch's defense attorney confined his interrogation to eliciting that each witness indeed believed that Franch could make gas out of water. And that all of them would invest more money with Franch if they had more to invest. Even my expert witness, an eminent authority on internal combustion fuels, couldn't testify with absolute certainty that there wasn't some possible substance that could turn ordinary liquid into a form of fuel.

The judge directed a verdict of not guilty.

The witnesses were overjoyed at the outcome. At least one of the jurors sought out Franch and invested himself.

And yet my biggest surprise came when I told Coleman that Franch had been acquitted. "I'm sorry," I said. "I really didn't think it would come out this way."

"Son," Coleman said, "don't feel bad. I figured this would happen."

"How did you figure that?" I asked.

"Because the son of a bitch can do it. He can make gas out of water."

With that, Coleman patted my shoulder, turned, and left the courthouse.

Years later, Franch was tried and convicted for selling more than 100 percent of the "invention." True enough, he probably sold about 5,000 percent. Whatever percentage the investor wanted was fine with Franch. He received probation on the condition that he discontinue his sales activities.

Franch died a pauper a few years ago. America lost a real gem. For all his deceitfulness, he sold hope, and undeniably, his investors loved him for it.

WILLIAM J. BAUER
JUDGE, UNITED STATES COURT OF APPEALS
FOR THE SEVENTH CIRCUIT
CHICAGO, ILLINOIS

The Bitch Set Me Up

I WAS APPOINTED BY THE COURT TO REPRESENT AN INDIGENT defendant charged with bank robbery. The prosecution had considerable evidence that my client was one of the three robbers, but my man insisted on a trial, since it cost him nothing.

The prosecution's chief witness was my client's live-in girlfriend, who had apparently seen him remove weapons, rope, and a bank bag from the back of his car a day or two after the robbery.

When she was called to the stand, I raised with the judge the testimonial privilege that prohibits one spouse from testifying against the other. The judge reminded me that my client and his girlfriend were just that—friends and not spouses. Ah, but, I said to the judge, perhaps I can prove that my client and the woman lived so closely together, effectively as man and wife, that they enjoyed a common-law marriage. That would prevent her from testifying. Could I question the lady preliminarily on this point before the prosecution attempted to elicit damning testimony from her? The judge sighed, signaling his impatience with me, but said, yes, you may proceed. So I did.

In response to my questioning, the lady admitted that she and the defendant had lived together for more than a year. Occasionally she was introduced as his "old lady." Yeah, she said, she and the defendant had a joint checking account. I was about to move in for the kill when my client summoned me over to counsel table, where he was sitting watching all of this.

As I leaned over, my client whispered, "What the hell are you doing? What if the judge decides we're married? I don't want to be married to this bitch!"

I was uncertain exactly how to address his concern except to suggest that he worry about that later. But the prospect of marriage to this lady troubled him more than what I would have considered an immediate problem of somewhat greater potential distress. My client pressed his inquiry. Before too long the already impatient judge summoned me back to the podium. When I arrived the court notified me that he would complete my interrogation of the lady. After a well-placed question or two from the judge ("Now, ma'am, you don't consider yourself a married woman, do you?" "No, Your Honor"), the judge ruled that there was no common-law marriage. The woman would testify.

My client was convicted and got twenty-five years. I must say, he seemed to take the verdict in stride.

Maybe he was relieved that he didn't have to get divorced as well.

PETER B. BRADFORD
CONNER & WINTERS
OKLAHOMA CITY, OKLAHOMA

When Irish Eyes Are Smiling

In the courts of England, barristers plead their cases with a degree of formality seen in few other places. Our lawyers wear wigs and robes, as do the judges. Our judicial system is a part of the great history of our country. It exists today much as it did hundreds of years ago. There are times, though, when a little informality goes a long way.

A few years ago, as I sat in court awaiting my own client's case to be heard, I watched an Irish advocate (let us call him O'Brien) appear before the court in the Old Bailey, the principal criminal court in the United Kingdom. O'Brien was defending a man who had pleaded guilty to a vicious attack in which he had taken a broken bottle to the victim's face and inflicted dreadful injuries.

The judge that day was the feared Mr. Justice Thessiger, now dead, but in his day a terrifyingly harsh and unsympathetic jurist. O'Brien, unaccustomed to the excessively formal coded language used by barristers when addressing the court, with its florid speech and etiquette (or well aware of it, yet cleverly deciding to risk a different approach all the better to serve his client), addressed the judge.

"My Lord," O'Brien began in his lilting Irish way, "I've heard a great deal about you, and they tell me you are a fair man."

The English barristers and others sitting in the courtroom, to a man (and woman), held their breaths. O'Brien's opening gambit—with its Irish pub informality and friendly intimacy—brought such a silence that had a pin dropped it would have been heard throughout the kingdom.

But O'Brien was not deterred by the silence.

"As I see it, my Lord," he continued, now as "Irish" as ever, "'tis me job to see if we can agree together on the number of years in prison my client is going to get."

From up on high Mr. Justice Thessiger peered over the top of his glasses and down on O'Brien standing before him patiently waiting. Not a few barristers in the courtroom noticeably cringed, much as one does when viewing an unavoidable accident about to happen.

The old judge said nothing at first. And then a slight smile appeared at the corners of his mouth. Spectators later described it as if a small crack had opened in the frozen tundra. Then, in a quiet voice, the judge spoke.

"Mr. O'Brien," the judge said, "in point of fact I was thinking somewhere on the *lighter* side of ten years' imprisonment as a suitable punishment for your client."

With this, O'Brien shook his head in bewilderment, and then with a broad smile on his face and a gleam in his eye he retorted, "My Lord, I knew we was years apart, but I never for a moment thought they was *light-years.*"

The old judge couldn't contain his mirth. O'Brien's client received what anyone would agree was leniency, whereupon O'Brien thanked the judge and left the courtroom.

On his way out O'Brien was seen to smile at the other wigged and robed barristers awaiting their turns before the feared Mr. Justice Thessiger.

CHRISTOPHER SALLON QC
DOUGHTY STREET CHAMBERS
LONDON, ENGLAND

Hidden Justice

A YEAR OR SO AFTER MY "SALT AND PEPPER" CASE, BY THEN a more "seasoned" prosecutor (sorry about that, just couldn't resist), I teamed up with another assistant United States attorney on a new case. The new prosecution was in front of one of the most respected and, indeed, fairest and best judges on our court's bench—respected, fair, but so peculiar in his courtroom habits that he had become a legend in his own time.

Ask most lawyers who regularly appear in court and they'll tell you about one particular judge who is known for his or her weird behavior. Maybe it's that the bench attracts more than its fair share of eccentrics. More likely, I think, is the fact that the courts of our country mirror the general population. Most of us can point to a strange but nonetheless lovable aunt, or uncle, or friend, or coworker, and so on. Anyway, as I said, this particular judge was smart, and hardworking and fair. But to call him eccentric was an understatement. On occasion, he would drive the lawyers who appeared before him absolutely batty.

My colleague and I were in court. I was seated at counsel's table watching as he stood before the lectern addressing the court. The defense attorney in this case had filed a motion asking that the judge throw the case out of court because of what he contended was a fatal legal flaw in the way the defendant, his client, had been charged. The defense attorney had just finished his argument. He had done a good job. His point—which he made effectively—was that his client's guilt or innocence was beside the point. The case should not proceed to trial before a jury because we the prosecutors had not charged him in the way that the law required.

We had decided that my colleague would argue this point for the prosecution, and so there he stood, ready to rebut the points that the defense lawyer had made and convince the judge that the government had indeed filed its charges properly, in accordance with the law.

Now, this prosecutor was an impressive guy. He had graduated top of his class from Harvard, had clerked for a justice on the United States Supreme Court, and was generally known in our office as a rising star. His dogged preparation, when combined with his superior intellect, made him a real match for any adversary—or for any judge, for that matter. This judge was also of superior intellect, a Harvard Law man himself, and someone who read every brief, every case cited to him by counsel. I sat back in my chair, eagerly awaiting what I assumed would be a challenging duel of wits between the young prosecutor and the judge. Instead, I and the rest of the courtroom were treated to an episode that could have been written for *I Love Lucy* or maybe *Seinfeld.* And though, to this day, I really believe that we had charged the defendant properly, as the law required, it was the egg salad that had as much to do with the case's outcome as any lofty legal principles.

The case had been called by the judge at about 11:30 A.M., so that by the time the defense attorney had finished his argument and the prosecution got its turn, it was pushing noon. The young prosecutor was just getting into his presentation to the court, his really important points about to be made, when all of a sudden the judge's head dipped below the bench, completely out of view of those seated in the courtroom. And then, just as suddenly as it had disappeared, up again it popped. There he was again, in his distinguished black robes, his glasses perched on his nose, his thick wavy gray hair adding to the image of this very impressive jurist. But then, a few seconds later, the judge's head popped out of sight, only to reemerge after a short while.

When it happened a third time, my colleague, still standing before the judge, articulating his argument, without breaking stride, looked over in my direction. Can you fucking believe this? his eyes said. Then he turned back to the bench, just in time for the judge's next nosedive.

But as I said, this young prosecutor was a real smart fellow. He figured it out. He's got it, knows what's going on up there. So he continues with his argument, as though nothing unusual at all is happening on the bench. He is in the midst of making a very important point. In fact, he is saying to the court, "And, Your Honor, the most important legal point for the court's consideration is . . ."

Just then, down again goes the judge's head—way down, below the bench. As soon as the judge is completely submerged, the young prosecutor stops speaking in midsentence. The air in the courtroom is still. Not a sound is heard. No one seems even to be breathing. The young prosecutor stands before the lectern and waits. Silence rapidly fills up space. The judge's head is still down there; he's doing whatever he's doing. But now he begins to realize that something is wrong up top, nothing is happening. No one is speaking. He can't just stay down. So he raises his head, like a soldier in a trench, fearful of an oncoming bullet.

The judge's mouth is full. He's been down there furtively eating his lunch. He pretends that nothing unusual is going on. He nods at the young prosecutor, his mouth clearly full, stuffed with the sandwich he has been gobbling belowdecks. He nods again, feigning normalcy, indicating silently to the prosecutor that he is to continue with his argument, finish the important sentence he was in the midst of uttering. But the prosecutor remains silent. He's a statue standing there, facing the judge, across the lectern. His face is blank, completely expressionless. He waits. Silence bears down on the courtroom like a tidal wave rolling to shore, visible now, but the inevitable deafening roar still too far away to be heard. Someone is going to have to speak. But the prosecutor waits. And then it happens.

The judge opens his mouth. He tries to pocket the half-chewed bits of sandwich inside his cheeks. "Continue, Counsel," he says. But as he does so, fragments of mushy white bread, accompanied by globs of egg salad, spew out toward his bench, splattering his papers like airborne pigeon droppings. The remainder of the egg salad slides down his lips, covering his chin and flecking onto his black robe like sequins on a ball gown. The judge knows he can't even wipe at his chin. He pretends the unpretendable. "Continue," he repeats to the prosecutor, as though nothing out of the ordinary has happened.

The young prosecutor speaks again. He finishes his sentence. Then he delivers what I know is a very abbreviated version of his argument. Within less than three minutes he's finished. He stands before the judge.

"Defense motion denied. The prosecution goes forward," the judge announces, egg salad still oozing its way from his chin to his robe. He grabs his gavel. "Court adjourned," he announces as he rises from the bench and heads for the small door to his left, which will permit escape into his chambers and paper towels.

"Thank you, Your Honor," the young prosecutor says to the judge's rear view, as he collects his papers and returns to counsel's table. Our eyes meet.

That's that, he smiles at me.

For years afterward I would see the judge in a local café around the corner from the courthouse. Eating egg salad.

R.L.

Disorder in the Court IV

MR. RAYES: Your Honor, I have a short witness, and Mr. Dyer has agreed to take him out of order.

THE COURT: How short?

MR. RAYES: It is Mr. Long.

THE COURT: No problem with interrupting?

MR. DWYER: Not at all, Your Honor.

THE COURT: Put Long on.

MR. DWYER: As long as he is short.

THE COURT: Defendant is remanded to the custody of the sheriff, who is ordered to carry into execution the order of the court.

THE DEFENDANT: Judge, can I say something?

THE COURT: Sure.

THE DEFENDANT: Did you say, "Executed"?

THE COURT: No. You got thirty years, Mr. Ashford.

THE COURT: What's the problem?

THE BAILIFF: Oh, a cockroach was on the exhibit table, Your Honor.

PLAINTIFF'S COUNSEL: Motion to quash.

THE COURT: Granted.

MR. LAVIN: My objection is I would prophylactically object to any question—

THE COURT: Prophylactically?

Mr. Lavin: I am not talking about preventing contraception, Judge. I am talking about preventing the line of questioning that would be outside the scope of—

The Court: Your prophylactic objection is premature.

Mr. Lavin: I will withdraw it.

A Good Judge

ONE OF THE BEST JUDGES IN TELLER COUNTY, COLORADO, never received a law degree.

Margaret Tekavee was born in Austria in 1912 and grew up in Victor, Colorado, the daughter of a miner. She entered first grade unable to speak English. When she graduated from high school, facing limited employment opportunities as a woman and with no family funds for higher education, she obtained secretarial work and eventually got a job as county clerk. When the justice of the peace, Vincent Ryan, retired in 1955, Margaret convinced the county commissioners to let her serve as both judge and clerk on an interim basis until the next election. She ran for the office and won, and continued to get overwhelming support for election each subsequent time she ran. Margaret educated herself on the law using her lunch hour each day to pore through cases in the courthouse library.

Judge Tekavee was required to retire in 1984 at the age of seventy-two, after serving as Teller County judge for almost thirty years. In a 1992 interview she was asked if she ever suffered the burnout frequently complained about by today's legal professionals. Her response was emphatic.

"Never! I loved the law. I read it, I breathed it and drank it." When asked if she was ever led astray by a formally educated attorney appearing in her court, she said, "Once in a while an attorney would kind of trip me up, but that'd be the last time."

The following excerpt written by Colorado Springs attorney Robert B. Murray speaks volumes about the character of Margaret Tekavee and local attorney Sam Nikkel and what it was like to practice in Cripple Creek in the mid-fifties.

When I began to practice law in Colorado Springs in 1955, my small savings did not place me in a position to select my clients. Consequently, when the president of a very undercapitalized mining corporation sought my services, I agreed to represent his corporation before he had a chance to fully explain to me the nature of his problem.

He related to me that his company owned a mine in the Cripple Creek area, and although it was of doubtful value, he was attempting to get the mine on a paying basis by contracting with a group of miners to remove ore "by the foot." This was a common arrangement in our area, which meant simply that the miners did not work as employees but were paid by the foot of material removed. When the date arrived for them to be paid, a dispute about the amount had arisen between my new client and the miners.

It became my job to represent the company and attempt to negotiate a figure that the company would agree to pay and that the miners would accept. Negotiate as I would, the parties to the growing dispute could not agree. As a last resort, the miners retained their own attorney, the late Sam Nikkel, who was the only attorney in Cripple Creek at the time.

Sam was not one to waste his time negotiating if he felt that this procedure would not produce results. He promptly filed a suit that asked for the maximum amount to which the miners could possibly have been entitled. The suit was filed in the Teller County Court in Cripple Creek. The judge there was a woman, Margaret Tekavee.

Being quite familiar with the critical attitude that many Cripple Creek citizens possessed toward the Colorado Springs mining companies, the president of my corporate client was worried. He was aware that the judge and all the members of any jury that would be selected in the case undoubtedly knew the miners, because Cripple Creek was no longer the roaring gold camp of the past but was a friendly little town where everyone knew each other. Believing that a fair trial was impossible, he asked if I would try to change the trial site to Colorado Springs.

Remembering my duties to not permit my client to be "hometowned," I agreed. I got out the law books and went to work. When I completed my research, I was well satisfied that I had ample grounds to move the trial. I filed a motion for change of venue and it was set on the docket for oral argument.

When the day to hear the motion arrived, I argued with the confidence that only a young, inexperienced attorney is able to exhibit. I had one case I thought was a clincher and I saved it for the end. Then I quoted from it extensively to show that it was just about on all fours with the facts then before the court, and that under its finding, this case should be transferred to my client's city.

Mr. Nikkel then gave his argument. He based it almost solely on the assumption that it would be unfair to force all of the miners involved to go all the way to Colorado Springs to get their money.

Following the arguments, Judge Tekavee looked down from the bench directly at me. She began to speak in a pleasant voice. "Mr. Murray, I am sure you understand that your argument this morning was quite technical. You realize I am sure that we are a small community and that, therefore, I am not legally trained, at least I do not have any formal legal education. When confronted with a legal problem as involved as this trial, it is my custom to consult with our county attorney. Of course, you are aware of the fact that we have just one attorney here, so he is our county attorney also." She paused. Only then did I understand the import of her words. She turned to Mr. Nikkel. "Sam, will you approach the bench, please?"

My disappointment at that point was impossible to describe. I felt like objecting, but how could I base an objection on the fact that the judge was consulting with the county attorney? I wondered concernedly whether I was going to receive a firsthand illustration as to what "hometowning" was.

County Attorney Nikkel went to the bench. He and Judge Tekavee spoke softly, but I could hear them quite clearly. "Well, Sam, what do you think?" the judge asked while looking down at the attorney from the bench.

"Margaret," the county attorney began slowly, while thoughtfully rubbing his hand across his chin, "I think he's got me. You better find for him."

"All right, Sam, if that is what you think."

Mr. Nikkel took his seat. Judge Tekavee looked down from the bench. "The motion for change of venue filed by the defendant is granted."

Mr. Nikkel, now counselor to the miners, rose to his feet. "I feel that this finding is unfair to these people," he said. He turned and left the courtroom.

Quite bewildered with the whole proceeding, I remained seated at the attorney's table. Judge Tekavee stood to leave. She glanced at me with a very kindly, almost motherly look. "I hope you have nice weather for your drive back to the Springs," she said.

JOHN W. SUTHERS, ESQUIRE
EXECUTIVE DIRECTOR
COLORADO DEPARTMENT OF CORRECTIONS
COLORADO SPRINGS, COLORADO

The Supremes

How did a nice Jewish boy like me end up being screamed at by the United States Supreme Court?

I represented the defendant at his criminal trial. He was convicted. We appealed. We lost. We kept on appealing and now here we were in front of the highest court in the land.

At trial our only defense was insanity. There was no question the defendant killed the victim. Throughout the trial I had referred to the victim as a despicable drug dealer, but his girlfriend tried to soft-pedal this by saying he sold drugs only infrequently. But that's like being almost pregnant: either you are or you aren't—and he was.

Despite this fact, the public service defense (getting rid of a bad guy) wouldn't work. The SODDI defense (some other dude did it) was out. And the TODDI defense (this other dude did it) wouldn't work either.

I was stuck with insanity as a defense.

Insanity and I are old friends (right after sex, drugs, and rock 'n' roll), but a little insanity wouldn't work. I needed *big insanity*. I thought I had the raw material. My client was a paranoid schizophrenic. He had been hearing voices of God, St. Peter, and Satan, sometimes all at once, like they were some kind of trio. Also, he thought JFK and Marilyn Monroe were his parents and that the victim in question was trying to kill him by squirting his AIDS-infected blood on the cocaine before he sold it.

These were clearly "insane" facts. Under normal circumstances, my client could communicate these delusions to the jury with fervor and conviction (I hate that word). But the zombie sitting next to me at counsel's table was so chemically cauterized, he appeared to the jury as synthetically sane.

He was convicted and sentenced to death. I appealed to the Nevada Supreme Court. The argument was lively, the decision was delayed. I was beginning to have hope. Then *pow*, a 4–1 decision affirming the conviction.

I wasn't ready to give up. I was appointed to file a petition of certiorari to the U.S. Supreme Court, the last chance for romance. Incredibly, the court granted certiorari. The case would be heard.

At this time a coalition of disparate organizations contacted me and offered their help. Four groups, the American Psychiatric Association, the National Association of Criminal Defense Lawyers, the Nevada Attorneys for Criminal Justice, and the Coalition for the Free (that one was for equal rights for ex-patients—I'm not making this up, it exists) filed supporting briefs.

I went to three separate practice court procedures, in Philadelphia, New York, and Washington. I was ready! Bring on the court.

However, into every life a little rain must fall. The day before my argument, a water main in Washington broke. Unfortunately, this closed the building where I was preparing with my co-counsel. His firm arranged a suite in the Hay-Adams Hotel, an old elegant institution directly across from the White House. This suite cost $1,275 a day without a bathroom (I wonder what that would have cost?).

We arrived in court at the appointed time, 9:00 A.M. It was bitter cold outside. We were taken to a room by the clerk of the court who wore a morning coat and told us the do's and dont's:

Don't touch the microphone;
Don't hit the microphone while flipping the pages of your legal pad;
    and last but not least,
Don't address Justice O'Connor as Sandy Baby.

We entered the courtroom. I spread out my materials. I reviewed my opening and then it happened. I got nervous. Me, someone who has looked at the wrong end of a gun twice and who has seen crazy Charlotte (my mother—the best way to describe her is like General Patton wearing a skirt) eat Grape-Nuts without her teeth. I felt queasy. My throat was dry. My heart was pounding.

My case was called. I stood at the podium. My knees were actually shaking. I started speaking slowly, deliberately, purposefully. Suddenly, Justice Kennedy asked me a question and the nervousness dissipated.

The questions were coming fast and furious. Justice Scalia was especially intense. Almost rude. His questions pointed. The one that sticks in my mind was when he asked about a defendant putting on a clown suit.

Should that be evidence of insanity? I felt like saying, *Yes,* if he borrowed one of yours, your Bozo-ness. Instead, I tried my best to see where he was going and answer convincingly. (I couldn't see where he was going. I answered anyway. What else is new?) It was the longest thirty minutes of my life. I was responding to the clown suit hypothetical when the red light went on and Chief Justice Rehnquist said thank you.

But my motor was still churning. Here I was, barreling down the highway at breakneck speed, my eyes darting between the road and the rearview mirror, and the red light goes off. Now, the rules of the Supreme Court are the rules of the Supreme Court. Red light means stop. It doesn't mean slow down. It doesn't mean, hey, Justice Rehnquist, hold up there a minute, I'm coasting in third gear here, give me a couple of minutes to slow down, I've got some more good stuff to say. I want to get back to that clown suit business for just a minute. Nope. When that red light clicks on, you've got to click off.

So I actually held my breath. I smiled in the direction of the court, you know, as though to say, Okay, Okay, I know the rules. I've stopped. And by the way, I'd like to thank all nine of you (including you, Sandy Baby) for letting me come up here and spend this quality time with you guys. But by then the members of the court had apparently erased me from their collective memory. As I was about to turn and walk from the podium, I could see that they were engaged in the shuffling of papers necessary to be ready for the next argument and the next lawyer to begin his or her argument of a lifetime.

So I gathered my materials, replaced them in my briefcase, and left. I felt as though I were walking on air. I was glowing as if I had finished the marathon. I'd been to the top of the mountain. It's hard to describe my feelings, but I believe this experience changed me. It's tough to explain.

And you know what?

The Supremes reversed the conviction.

MACE J. YAMPOLSKY, ESQUIRE
LAS VEGAS, NEVADA

My Two Trips to the Supreme Court

T WICE IN MY CAREER AS A LAWYER, I HAVE BEEN PRIVILEGED to present myself on official business to the U.S. Supreme Court.

Cash for Castro

My first trip to the Supreme Court was as a first-year associate at a prominent New York law firm.

My first day at work, the senior associate invited me out to my initiation lunch—in the dim subterranean cafeteria. "Bring a legal pad," he instructed.

Good thing I did. Because all he talked about was a lawsuit our firm was pursuing against Banco Nacional de Cuba—now wending its way through tippety-top legal channels to none other than the justices who sit on the Supreme Court in Washington. And I was to have a part.

My parents just about fainted.

"My daughter!" my father said, weeping. "Working on a U.S. Supreme Court case!"

I slaved. I sweated. I stayed at the office till 4:00 A.M., checking footnotes, case cites, arguments, and everything else a first-year associate knows how to check. We got the brief done and submitted on time. Months passed. It was time for the case to be heard.

My esteemed firm would not fly me to Washington. After all, I wasn't arguing the case, was I? But since I had written Footnote number 5 in the brief, they would send me by train.

The more senior associates told me sternly what to do. I was to dress in the most restrained, respectful, sober black suit I could possibly find. I went to Bloomingdale's and explained the situation to the suit lady, who sat down and cried. We scratched our heads. I left carrying the most lifeless, dreary item of gray clothing I have ever owned. "Have fun," the saleslady croaked, "at the U.S. Supreme Court!"

I sweated the whole train ride to Washington, seriously hoping I'd done nothing wrong in my footnote. The case involved Cuba's nationalizing of foreign assets during the revolution decades before, resulting in the seizing of funds at what was now a major New York bank. It was shocking. It was an outrage. After all those years, they still hadn't given it back! And Cuba claimed (my memory is a bit fuzzy now) that the Banco Nacional, which somehow got mixed up with the money, was an "alter ego" of the Cuban government—and therefore immune from suit, because of sovereign immunity.

It was the job of Footnote 5 to help prove that the bank was *not* an alter ego and *could* be sued. Or that the government of Cuba *could* be sued and the bank *was* part of the government, I can't now remember which.

But that day I knew. And Footnote 5 had a role to play. I imagined the bespectacled justices peering over the brief. "Footnote 5," I could hear them intone, "Footnote 5 carries the day!" My heart pounded. On the other hand, what if I'd botched the whole thing?

Before leaving New York, I had been carefully instructed to go to the Counsel's Room in the Supreme Court and wait there for other lawyers from my firm. "Do not," I was told, "go into the courtroom like a member of the ordinary public!"

I got there hours early. I sat. I squirmed. I waited. I was about to burst like an exploding cigar. Because our case was to be heard in fifteen minutes! What would the venerables back in New York say when they heard I went to the Supreme Court and missed the argument? I shot out to the information office and got a rush pass.

Inside the mahogany chambers, I saw our lawyers' group in the very front row. For goodness' sake! Why hadn't they come and gotten me? I sat in my seat, constrained in my gray, tightly buttoned, puritanical garb—and noticed the other associates were cheerfully dressed.

"Where have you been?" they asked. Just as the clerk called our case.

It all flew by faster than the Cuban Revolution. There was our stately senior partner, an experienced Supreme Court practitioner, with handlebar mustache and practically older than all the justices combined. He rose to face the bench, elegantly bringing all arguments to bear to make our case.

He orated. He didn't hem or haw once. We just about slugged Cuba to banana bits.

We won the case.

And apparently Footnote 5 had nothing to do with it.

The Court Considers Chocolate

My second trip to the U.S. Supreme Court was as a member of the press.

As legal correspondent for *The Art Newspaper,* an international monthly, I got myself a press seat the moment the Supreme Court granted certiorari in a First Amendment case questioning a "decency" consideration in federal art grants.

The case, *National Endowment for the Arts v. Karen Finley,* involved a performance artist whose work included the onstage smearing of her seminude body with chocolate, while uttering, "God is death."

Apparently, Congress was mad she had wasted good chocolate. But actually, the dispute arose because the National Endowment for the Arts had funded exhibits of homoerotic photographs by Robert Mapplethorpe, and a photo by Andrès Serrano of a crucifix in his own urine. Outraged, Congress passed a law making the NEA consider decency in making art grants.

Four artists challenged the law as unconstitutional, saying it discriminated against disfavored speech such as chocolate-smearing. The government said the First Amendment doesn't apply when it is choosing which art to fund.

It was now 1998. With two young kids, I had placed law firm practice on hold, and taken up legal journalism on the side. I lived in Boston and hadn't been to the Supreme Court in years.

"Imagine!" my father said, weeping. "My daughter, in the U.S. Supreme Court!"

"She went once before," my mother reminded him.

And I was going again by train. But I treated myself to an overnight berth, to ensure a full night's rest.

I boarded my compartment. I put my feet up. I studied and restudied the briefs. I noted the holes in each side's arguments, and wondered how

I would tell the justices apart for my quotes. Brain spinning, I turned out the light and settled in.

Which was when the trouble began. Because as the dark, thundering, speeding conduit barreled me in the night toward the Supreme Court and history, something was wrong with my mattress. Which was evidently a heating pad—concentrated on a most inopportune spot. Where it was slowly stewing my posterior.

I tossed. I floundered. I roasted my derriere. I barely slept a wink, riding the final hour in a delicately toasted condition, standing up to alleviate the distress. I arrived at Union Station at daybreak—with an excruciating aversion to sitting down.

At the Press Room, I got my seat assignment. Thrilled, I entered the courtroom.

Fate had brought me back. The final appeal had arrived. I had mastered the briefs in their complexity. I had journeyed all the way to the U.S. Supreme Court to see what would happen to national arts funding, and my place in history was waiting for me.

On a bare wooden seat.

Gingerly, I sat.

But I rose above the agony of the moment. The case was announced. The argument was exhilarating. I could follow every twist and turn. The Supreme Court must be really progressing. They peppered the lawyers with questions, barely letting them speak. Confoundingly, after hundreds of pages of briefs exhaustively arguing free-speech rights, it appeared the court might decide the case on very narrow grounds—whether the artists had suffered enough damage to be in court at all. It was an astonishing turn of events.

I sighed when it was over. For the many who wanted to strike the decency law from the books, the case might be a disappointment. But I had great quotes from the justices. Like other members of the press, I now knew them intimately by the backs of their heads.

I spent the day sight-seeing in Washington. In the afternoon, I stopped in to see the Supreme Court lobby exhibits on my way back to the station. And promptly stubbed my toe on the steel grate that slams down on the gift shop at closing.

But I didn't sue the justices. Nope, I figured they had enough to worry about already, with the chocolate-smearing, First Amendment decency case. I got on the train home.

I had a terrific story.

I had a stubbed toe and a sore you-know-what.

I was completely satisfied.

MARTHA B. G. LUFKIN, ESQUIRE
LINCOLN, MASSACHUSETTS

Court Time

A PETITION HAD BEEN FILED WITH THE COURT BY DEFENSE counsel in a civil suit for the production of some photographs that related to the case. The other side objected to turning them over, so the judge permitted oral argument on the point.

The objecting attorney said, "Your Honor, I took those photographs myself. Now, since I'm the attorney of record for the plaintiff in this case, those photos are protected by the attorney work product doctrine. They're clearly privileged from production to the other side in this lawsuit."

It had been a long day. The judge had heard many motions. There were many more to go. He looked down at the lawyer.

"When you argue before me, you're a lawyer. When you take pictures, you're a photographer. Turn over the pictures."

The lawyer was stunned. "Your Honor," he demanded, "I'd like to argue that at length."

"You just did," replied the judge, rapping his gavel and calling the next case.

HARRY B. BAINBRIDGE
BAINBRIDGE LAW OFFICES
FLOSSMOOR, ILLINOIS

A Judge's Mailbox

L AWYERS SPEND THEIR ENTIRE PROFESSIONAL LIVES SPEAK-
ing and writing on behalf of others. It is not surprising, then, that the U.S.
Postal Service ranks lawyers among its most frequent users of first-class
mail. I'll bet there is no other profession in the world—except, perhaps,
for Vanna White's—in which letters play such an integral part.

Judges get their share of letters, too.

It has been said that whenever a judge makes a decision, one side
thinks he's wrong, and the other side thinks he's right, but for the wrong
reason. That pretty well summarizes the general tenor of letters to a judge.

For example, a woman disappointed with the outcome of her divorce
case began her two-page letter to me as follows:

> My dear Judge Silverman:
>
> I do solemnly swear that you are undoubtedly the biggest unmitigated
> asshole a merciful God ever put upon the face of this earth. Where in
> the hell did you come from? Out of the slime? How did someone so
> stupid as you get to be a judge? I swear, you are dumber than even a
> bankruptcy judge.
>
> You are vile, contemptible trash, a mockery to justice and law and
> an embarrassment to this land. As this holiday season draws near, I
> wish you had never been born.

Then the letter went on to become insulting.

I once heard a dispute between the owner of a small Apache Junction
motel, and one of his tenants—Mrs. Jones, I'll call her—who operated a
dog-grooming business on the premises. At the conclusion of the trial, I

ordered Mrs. Jones, among other things, to make reasonable efforts to keep her clients' dogs from "fouling the common areas."

About a month after the trial, I received this handwritten letter from the plaintiff:

> On October 11, 1986, at approximately 4:30 p.m., one of Mrs. Jones's customers (pardon my French, Your Honor) "made No. 2" on the sidewalk right in front of the Laundromat. Will you please write me back right away and tell me what you are planning to do about it?

What was *I* planning to do about it? I wasn't planning to do *anything* about it. I wrote him back, but sidestepped the issue. I hope he did the same.

Judge Sylvan Brown received this letter from a prospective juror in a criminal case whom he had excused from the panel sua sponte (from the Latin "of its own accord"; in this case, on the court's own initiative):

> Although being spared the inconvenience of jury duty does not displease me, I wish to register with you my strongest objections to the crude and peremptory manner in which you rejected me yesterday as a prospective juror in the Castillo case. . . . I will *not* sit quietly by when expected to acquiesce in the incredible claim that a defendant does not have to prove himself innocent.
>
> I do not have to have statements reworded so that I can understand them; I understand what is meant by the presumption of innocence. I consider it a superb example of legal mythmaking and specious reasoning.
>
> You have no reason whatsoever, not even an implied one, for rejecting me and I consider both your action and your rude behavior an insult at once to my integrity, my intelligence and my impartiality.

The letter showed copies sent to the governor, the chief justice, the attorney general, and *60 Minutes*.

Someone I'll call Alma Jane Smith once wrote to me to complain about the provision in her decree requiring her former husband to make his child support payments through the clerk of the court.

Now, look—

> I, Alma Jean Smith, do NOT want my husband, Lynn Smith, to mail my check to *YOU!* You got that? I want him to pay me direct so I get the money without getting jerked around!

Judge Robert Hertzberg sent me a letter he received from a *pro se* defendant—one who chose to defend himself—whom he had sentenced to prison. That fellow wrote to him, in part:

> I'm going to appeal, and upon remand you will be permitted a second opportunity to violate my rights, but this time I will be fully prepared and you can count on that! Your theory that I utilized the situation to my advantage is in my opinion such a fantasy and respectfully, you're full of shit!

His conviction was respectfully affirmed by the court of appeals.

Judge Frank Galati was the recipient of this letter from a woman I'll call Sue Green at whose request he had issued a domestic relations order of protection three days earlier:

> I, Sue Green, wish to withdraw my order of protection against Billy Joe Green.
>
> My husband and a few family members thought that if he could get me really upset, then that would be a good way to get me out of the house for the weekend so that he could surprise me with new furniture. Being that I am so emotional, they didn't know that I would take their joke so honestly. Sorry.

That scenario reminded Judge Galati of something Ricky Ricardo and Fred Mertz once tried to pull on Lucy.

My favorite letter came from a guy I'll call Ronald R. Roe, a man sentenced to prison for child molestation. He wrote to me complaining that the Department of Corrections had given him a higher security classification than he felt he deserved.

It was a typical inmate letter. He recited myriad mitigating factors the prison administration had supposedly overlooked in his case.

What was unusual about the letter was not the content but the stationery on which it was written. The letter was typed on expensive-looking personalized letterhead that reads as follows:

FROM THE DESK OF. . .

RONALD R. ROE

No. 851009

ARIZONA STATE PRISON COMPLEX
10,000 SOUTH WILMOT ROAD
TUCSON, ARIZONA 85777-0004

"From the *desk* of Ronald R. Roe"? To be accurate, it should have said, "From the *cell* of Ronald R. Roe," but that doesn't really matter. The point is, a guy with personalized stationery like that probably gets as many letters as I do.

BARRY G. SILVERMAN
JUDGE, UNITED STATES COURT OF APPEALS
FOR THE NINTH CIRCUIT
PHOENIX, ARIZONA

Hottest Lawyer in Town

I LIVE AND PRACTICE LAW IN CUT BANK, MONTANA, POPULA-
tion 3,329.

Our district judge travels a circuit and so holds court in our town only
two days a month. Matters pile up, and the courtroom is usually crowded
with town folk when court is in session. That was certainly true on that
summer Tuesday, the day I won't soon forget. Unfortunately, neither will
my friends and neighbors.

I had been at the bench arguing for an uncontested divorce on behalf of
my client. An easy case. The judge granted the divorce. I grabbed the file and
quickly turned to leave the courtroom. In doing so I accidentally bumped
against the railing that separates the judge's bench from counsel tables.

I thought I saw a cloud of dust come from the railing. That did strike
me as unusual—the courtroom was kept immaculately clean. Then I felt
an uncomfortably warm feeling on my leg. Flames shot from my pants
pocket. It seems that when I bumped the bench I had somehow ignited a
book of matches in my pocket. By now the entire packed courtroom was
watching, including the judge.

As I tried nonchalantly to pat out the fire, another pack of matches in
the same pocket ignited. I frantically beat down the flames and then, cool
as you please, I turned to the judge.

In the interest of public safety, I said, I think I'll be leaving the building. The judge said he thought that was a good idea.

I do get asked about that incident from time to time.

I tell my friends and neighbors that something like that was bound to
happen.

I am, after all, the hottest lawyer in town.

ROBERT G. OLSON
FRISBEE, MOORE & OLSON, P.C.
CUT BANK, MONTANA

Privacy, Please!

WHILE AWAITING MY TURN AT BAT ON BEHALF OF A CLIENT in the municipal court of Clinton, Arkansas, the judge called the case of a lady charged with wearing insufficient burnt orange–colored clothing in the woods during the height of deer hunting season. Such is a violation of law during deer season, particularly if you are armed with a deer rifle, as was the lady.

She pleaded not guilty and announced to the court that she would serve as her own attorney. (What we lawyers call acting *pro se*.) The district attorney called the local game warden as the state's first witness.

The game warden proceeded to tell the court he arrested the young lady because she was not legally attired to hunt deer. He explained that she did not display the necessary square inches of burnt orange clothing, and yet she was bearing arms, indicating she was out hunting. The prosecution then rested its case.

The young lady took the witness stand and proceeded to tell the judge her story. She said she was riding as a passenger in a pickup truck operated by her husband. While in the woods she told her husband to stop the vehicle, that she felt the call of nature.

The judge asked her why she needed a thirty-ought-six deer rifle to accomplish her purpose.

She responded, "Judge, you don't know these horny game wardens like I do."

PHIL STRATTON
ATTORNEY AT LAW
CONWAY, ARKANSAS

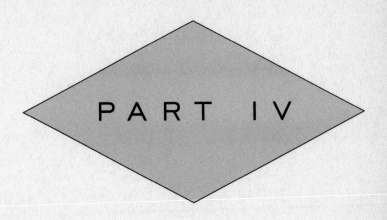

PART IV

LEFT FIELD

LIFE CAN BE AN ASSEMBLY LINE. THE SAME OLD, SAME OLD sets in. Same old breakfast, same old route to work, same old TV shows at night, same old phone conversation with your mother—over and over, and over again. And work can be worse. Like the guy on the assembly line, work can become repetitive, wearying, dull. It's true of lawyering too. But on occasion, wonderfully less true.

It's the human condition and the predicaments that our species manages to create for itself. When the situation becomes too much to handle, it falls onto the lawyer's desk. The benefit for us lawyers is that our lives of routine—preparing for court, going to court, winning or losing in court—get a swift kick in the pants. The wild wind gusts in from left field. We are called upon to do something out of the ordinary to serve the needs of our clients. If we do it well—or we are simply lucky enough not to mess it up—our clients benefit. If we don't . . . well, if we don't, it's depression city. An unhappy client. An unhappy lawyer. But in either event we get some mighty interesting stories to tell. Like the ones that follow.

Crazy Sadie

I WAS REPRESENTING A CENTRAL ILLINOIS MUNICIPALITY IN A case involving the discharge of a municipal employee for falsifying time records. Assigned to the graveyard shift at the public works garage, the employee was in the habit of going out on the town when he was supposed to be working. His supervisor had supposedly turned his back on these continuing infractions. Based on these reports, the city fired the employee and demoted the supervisor. The union representing the employees filed a grievance. As a result, a hearing was scheduled to determine whether the city had sufficient cause to do what it had done. For that I was called in to marshal the proof and present the city's case. The problem was, the proof was all hearsay and rumor.

When I first met with the city's officials I learned that an anonymous caller had reported that the employee had been repeatedly seen in a bar downtown, instead of at work, as his time card showed, on the nights in question. An anonymous caller? I asked. Is that what the case against the employee was based on? Well, yes, that and some other rumors, I was told. But one of the officials with whom I met, I'll call him Dave, said he had a pretty good idea who that caller was. He told me that he was fairly certain it was a woman, I'll call her Sadie, who had had a series of marriages and out-of-marriage relationships with municipal employees. She had a reputation for being a little eccentric, Dave said, although he didn't elaborate. Great, I thought, a case built on rumor, hearsay, and an anonymous caller who was a municipal employee groupie and "a little eccentric" to boot.

Let's find her, I suggested. No problem, I was told, everyone knows where Sadie lives.

So we jumped into the official's car and drove to a rural area. Driving along an old farm road, we came to a dirt driveway leading to an old farm-house and several worn-looking farm buildings. Even out of doors, the place smelled. As we drove up, we were greeted by several mangy, vicious-looking dogs, running alongside our car and barking ferociously. Neither Dave nor I made any attempt to get out of the car until a plainly dressed woman with worn features came out and shooed the dogs from the car. Keeping a wary eye on the dogs, we then accompanied her into the farmhouse.

Declining her offer of a beverage, and wondering what in the hell I was doing there, I began trying to interview the woman. She was very interested in talking, but not about anything I asked her. Every question seemed to lead her off on a tangent that had nothing to do with the reason for our visit. It didn't take long for her behavior to convince me that, even if she was the anonymous caller and did know something about the case, I wasn't about to learn it from her.

As I was trying to excuse myself so that we could get out of there, she decided I should have a tour of her house.

"Gee, thanks," I said, "but we really must get going."

That was when she told me that one of the things she was particularly keen on letting me see was the shotgun she kept under her bed in case she was visited by "unwelcome strangers." It was probably my imagination, but I thought she gave me a funny look when she said that.

I thanked her for her time, and checking my wristwatch as though it had just sounded an alarm, I told her we really had to go. That's when she asked the question that sent shivers down my spine.

"You're a lawyer, aren't you?" she asked. This was twenty minutes or so into my attempted interview of her for a law case. Oh my God, I thought. Out of the corner of my eye, I could sense Dave slowly moving toward the door. He wouldn't leave me here, I tried to assure myself. No, he wouldn't run to his car and leave me to the mercy of this crazy lady and her hidden shotgun. Would he?

"Yes, ma'am, I'm a lawyer," I said, trying to sound as calm and interested as I could under the circumstances. "Yes, a lawyer. A lawyer," I think I repeated once or twice more.

"I want to show you something," she said, as she disappeared into her bedroom. Dave and I exchanged glances the minute she disappeared. Now, don't even think of leaving me, my glance told him. Don't even think about it.

A few seconds later the woman reappeared, holding not her shotgun but a letter.

"This here's a letter from my husband's lawyer," she said.

Which husband? I thought. "Really?" I said.

"Take a look at this," she said, handing me the letter.

All my instincts told me to decline the offer and head for the door immediately. I had no doubt that Dave would be at my heels. Still, there was the matter of that shotgun, not to mention the pack of wolves outside masquerading as dogs.

So I read the letter.

The letter was part complaint and part accusation. But the part that I clearly recall was the lawyer's written accusation to her that she was damaging her former husband's reputation in the community (which I took to mean among the city's other municipal employees) by telling everyone who would listen the reason she preferred her then current municipal employee boyfriend to her estranged municipal employee husband.

"He is ten years younger and two inches longer," the letter quoted the woman as saying.

The woman held the dogs while we made our escape. Needless to say, she did not testify at the hearing.

DONALD W. ANDERSON
DANIELS, MAURO & PINSEL
WAUKEGAN, ILLINOIS

Money in All the Right Places

THE YOUNG INSURANCE SALESMAN WAS MORE IMPRESSED WITH Mrs. Craig's* money than her measurements. Had he worked alongside her at the Bank of England currency printing works, he might have felt differently. Because there she was known by one and all as the woman with the best and the biggest. . . . features of all the ladies who worked in the used currency destruction unit. But more about that in a moment.

Mrs. Craig and her husband, a part-time truck driver, had just told the young insurance salesman that they were interested in starting a savings plan. They wanted to invest in a bond.

"How much were you thinking of?" asked the salesman hesitantly.

"Quite a lot," answered Mrs. Craig's husband, looking approvingly at his sweet but plain-looking wife.

"Perhaps £1,000 [$1,500]?" ventured the salesman, fearful that he was pushing his luck.

"A bit more, actually," said Mr. Craig, again with an approving look at Mrs. Craig.

The salesman waited politely.

"Say £100,000," said Mr. Craig.

The salesman gulped. He did his best to stay calm, but his head was spinning as he tried to calculate his commission on the deal. That holiday with his girlfriend in the Caribbean looked like a reality at last.

"Wonderful, wonderful," said the salesman rubbing his hands one over the other in anticipation. He quickly reached into his briefcase for forms. "We just have to complete the paperwork," he said. "It's really quite simple."

He took the details of the couple's earnings and assets. Mr. Craig said he earned £1,000 per month, Mrs. Craig not much more. In the section of

*Not her real name.

the form headed "assets,", the young salesman wrote down exactly what Mr. Craig told him: "Very large amounts of cash available at any time." And as it turned out, this was no idle boast.

So, let's return to Mrs. Craig's job at the Bank of England.

Mrs. Craig had discovered how to take full advantage of her job in the old and used money destruction unit. In short, with the help of two accomplices, she had figured out how to beat the system. The used bills that were to be destroyed rather than placed back in circulation were stored in cages under lock and key. There were two separate keys, held by two different people. But Mrs. Craig had worked out a way of switching the locks en route to the incinerators so that the second key was no longer needed.

Out of sight of the security guards and the cameras, the cages were opened and Mrs. Craig stashed, say, £20,000 to £30,000 ($30,000 to $45,000) in her bra and panties. It was as simple as that, although she had to build up the amount of cash over time so that the increase in her "vital statistics" would be gradual, and therefore less remarkable. It wasn't long before this rather plain-looking woman became the object of nudges and admiring glances among her unsuspecting male coworkers. By the time the scheme was in full bloom, so to speak, Mrs. Craig was as much admired for her physical attributes as her obvious devotion to her job. At the end of each working day, Mrs. Craig would walk out of the gate, past many of her admirers, which included, of course, the security guards—her accomplices having first checked to make sure that she wasn't "bulging" in any unnatural places.

Everything went exceedingly well until Mr. and Mrs. Craig decided to start their savings plan by purchasing a bond from that young insurance salesman. Now, it wasn't so much the purchasing of the bond that attracted attention; it was the method of payment. Mr. Craig walked into the young insurance salesman's office and emptied a sports bag full of £100,000 ($150,000) of used bills onto the young man's desktop. While the young man seemed quite happy about this, his supervisor reported Mr. and Mrs. Craig to the authorities. Given that Mr. Craig was a truck driver and the couple was known to live in somewhat modest accommodations, it did not take the local constable long to figure out that there might be some possible connection between the sports bag full of cash and Mrs. Craig's work at the Bank of England.

Undercover inquiries were made by the police fraud squad, injunctions were obtained, and bank accounts were frozen. One of the accomplices confessed and served twelve months in prison. Extraordinarily, none of the others were prosecuted. There was no way to trace the bills, and no way of showing exactly how much had been stolen. The Crown Prosecution Service felt they could not prosecute with only circumstantial evidence and the uncorroborated confession of an accomplice.

This did not stop the Bank of England from launching a civil action to recover the stolen money. The trial proved to be a real entertainment, with a succession of witnesses competing to produce the least plausible explanation of how they came to have assets well beyond their earning power.

The star of the show was Mr. Craig. He testified that the money from the sports bag was not Mrs. Craig's, but his. He told the court that his life operated on a strictly cash basis. Everything he did was in cash.

"Cash, it's in me genes," he declared proudly to the court.

At least one spectator at the trial was overheard whispering, "In his wife's jeans, he means."

IAN TERRY
FRESHFIELDS
LONDON, ENGLAND

Who Wears the Pants?

Early in my career, I moved from Denver, Colorado, to Omaha, Nebraska, to take a job with a law firm that handled large municipal finance transactions. I hadn't been there long when the partner for whom I worked assigned me to handle his client's interests in a multimillion-dollar municipal financing transaction in New York. The mere thought of traveling to New York—ground zero for major finance—sitting in some ornate conference room with a bunch of supersophisticated lawyers, all intent on voraciously protecting the interests of their own clients, was daunting enough. What made it worse was that although I knew in theory what a closing on a transaction like this one looked like—with piles of documents subjected to microscopic scrutiny and large checks and wire transfer slips changing hands at the speed of light—I had never actually attended one of these. Fact was, it scared me to death. I was scared of being embarrassed by these senior Wall Street lawyers, scared of missing something important and screwing things up unmercifully for my boss's client. Why didn't my boss send someone with more experience, I wondered? To this day I don't know. But on to New York I went, my heart, and most of my breakfast, in my throat.

I knew that in handling closings of very large financial transactions, a "preclosing" (a kind of dress rehearsal) often takes place the day before the actual closing. And that's what was scheduled here. So as soon as I got to New York I took a cab to the offices of the law firm that would host the actual closing. As I was shown into the palatial conference room, I was intent on not dropping the box of documents I had brought with me, which was teetering precariously on my arms. I could already see my papers scattered in piles all over the Oriental carpet stretched over the shiny mahogany floor, and me crawling around on all fours, retrieving my documents from between the legs of the lawyers I would not even have had the chance to meet.

I managed to make it into the room and to the conference table without incident. I then met the other lawyers. Clearly the most senior of the group was a man I'll call Mr. Tipton, senior partner of one of New York's oldest and most prestigious law firms. I noticed that he had a box of documents with him, too. They were regally perched in an empty swivel chair he had evidently removed from around the conference table and placed directly behind the seat he intended to occupy. We shook hands. Mr. Tipton wasn't what I'd call unfriendly. His greeting was cordial enough, but he had a clear, unmistakable air of importance about him. He was a pro's pro, a king of closings, someone I could just see his firm's juniors treating with unswerving respect. Mr. Tipton was a large man, quite tall, and what I would politely call stout, especially around the middle.

It was time for all the lawyers to exchange papers. I wasn't sure what to do. Should I begin? Should I wait? I must admit that my principal goal was still to avoid making a fool of myself. I waited, frozen. But nothing seemed to be happening. Finally, Mr. Tipton announced that he would now retrieve his documents and pass them out. He stood, pushed his chair back, and turned to where his papers awaited him. And then, his pants dropped. I can't tell you how this happened because he was wearing a belt, and I do believe it was fastened around his admittedly corpulent belly. But drop they did, all the way down to his socks. The others in the room froze, clearly uncertain what to do, or say. Mr. Tipton casually reached down, pulled up his trousers, gave his belt an extra hitch, and then turned to his box and began passing out his documents without so much as a word about what had happened. No one else said anything either. We just went through our dry-run closing.

From that day on, I have never had a moment's fear or apprehension about conducting a closing. I have always kept my wits—and my trousers—about me.

JAMES B. DEAN
ATTORNEY AT LAW
DENVER, COLORADO

A Day in the Life

THE PRACTICE OF LAW DOES HAVE ITS MOMENTS.

Dog Day Afternoon

Mrs. Jones had managed to foil a robbery at the bank where she worked as a teller. To award her for her efforts she was given a bonus and a half day off work. She intended to go shopping and stopped by her home to pick up her checkbook, which she had left on her desk in the spare bedroom.

She was surprised to find her husband's car in the driveway when she pulled up, but nothing could have surprised her more than what she saw when she entered her den. There was her husband, stark naked, having sex with the family dog.

Mrs. Jones quite understandably sought a divorce. I was retained. Unfortunately, her husband's romantic behavior with this particular member of the family is not considered adultery under South Carolina law.

My client settled on a divorce on no-fault grounds. There was no dispute over custody of the pooch.

Your Cheatin' Heart

It began as a routine real estate closing. The couple in my conference room wanted to refinance their home. There we sat, 4:30 P.M., dead of summer, the air conditioning droning on as I reviewed the legal papers with them. I asked my clients (the "Smiths") for their drivers' licenses—all very routine. Mr. Smith handed his over cheerfully. Mrs. Smith said she had left hers in her purse out in the car, and could she bring it in at the end of the closing? Sure, I said. After all, this was so routine. I'd done hundreds of closings like this and I would not be disbursing checks until all the paperwork was completed.

While we were busy reviewing and signing documents, my secretary entered the conference room and asked if she could have a word with me. I looked up from the papers to tell her not now, we were busy, but the look on her face—not to mention her insistent nodding in the direction of my office—changed my mind. When she and I got back to my office, my secretary picked up my phone and, pointing it at me like a loaded pistol, told me the real Mrs. Smith was on the line. I cleared my throat and took the phone.

"Hello," I said.

"Is that bitch, tramp girlfriend of my husband's there?" the real Mrs. Smith asked.

I looked at my secretary. She shrugged. What now? she seemed to be asking.

"Hold on," I said to the real Mrs. Smith. "I'll put your husband on the line."

My secretary transferred the call to the conference room as I walked back down the hall. As I reentered I told Mr. Smith that the call was for him. When he picked up the phone, I took the closing papers from the table and left. Twenty minutes later I reentered what was then an empty conference room.

It seems that Mr. Smith was trying to refinance his home to pay for his girlfriend's increasingly lavish lifestyle. The real Mrs. Smith apparently didn't like the idea. The closing never occurred.

But some lawyer got himself another client in a divorce case, no doubt about that.

When in Rome . . .

Two Miami lawyers arrived in tiny Glover, South Carolina, for a drug-trafficking trial involving their clients, some serious drug dealers who had the bad luck to have been stopped and arrested on the interstate just outside of Glover, as they were headed up north with a van filled with cocaine. I was representing a codefendant. On the day of trial the two lawyers arrived at court wearing tropical white cotton, lightweight suits with unbuttoned collars and polyester ties. They also sported off-white soft leather shoes. Presiding over the trial was Judge Hartness (secretly called "Heartless Hartness" by certain members of the local bar). The judge was a retired marine officer from World War II and perhaps the most conservative judge on the South Carolina bench.

Judge Hartness took the bench, saw these two lawyers and how they were attired, and called them before him. When the two lawyers introduced themselves, Judge Hartness carefully looked them up and down and then ordered them to return to court at 2:00 P.M. properly attired in dark suits and suitable shoes. Before excusing them the judge said that if they were late or failed to appear properly attired, he would hold them in contempt of court. The fine would be $10 per minute until they were back before him looking like lawyers rather than their clients. He instructed that when the fine hit $1,500 he would then tack on a term of six months in jail.

At 1:00 P.M. the Glover town police were summoned to intervene in a dispute at the local men's clothier located across the street from the courthouse. It seems two members of the Florida bar were assaulting each other. The tailor could fit only one of them by 2:00 P.M., and they could not agree on which was to be served first.

When informed of the situation by the town sheriff, Judge Hartness adjourned court for the day for the sake of public safety.

WILLIAM K. SWOPE
SWOPE AND ASSOCIATES, P.A.
CHARLESTON, SOUTH CAROLINA

A Satisfied Customer

I T SHOULD HAVE BEEN AN EASY GUILTY PLEA. THE PROSECU-
tion had the defendant cold. He had been seen tampering with the mailbox and had been arrested a short while later with a stolen check in his
pocket. The government was offering a plea agreement that would not really worsen the defendant's position. By the time his case was called, he
was already in prison on an earlier conviction. He was offered "concurrent
time," eighteen months that would be served at the same time as his present sentence, and it would not extend his prison stay. I was a New Jersey
public defender then, and I was assigned the case. I had presented the
prosecutor's deal. The old man closed his ears, literally by plugging them
with his fingers like a stubborn child.

"You're my lawyer," he said. "I'm not taking any plea. We're going to
trial. Defend me."

Mr. B was seventy years old, wrinkled and wiry. He had a warm,
nearly toothless smile, which grew broader when he told me where he was
serving time—Clinton, the women's prison that reserved a few spaces for
old men, convicted politicians, bad cops, and even a forcibly retired
judge.

After several meetings with Mr. B, I started to get the picture. We
were beyond the bluffing stage. He did not have to bluster and pretend he
would not plead guilty to anything as part of a strategy to get the most favorable plea bargain. We were at the bottom line and we both knew it. I realized that he would not plead guilty even if straight probation were
offered. It all boiled down to this: He was old, and prison—particularly a
women's prison—looked a whole lot better to him than the freedom of
homelessness on the streets, which is what he had before his last conviction.

The judge was irate because the defendant was insisting on a jury trial. He had better things to do with his court time than to take two long days trying this nonsense. The court had no time for this crazy old defendant or the softhearted public defender who could not pull a guilty plea out of him.

The trial was uneventful; everybody pretty much knew the script. The arresting officer's testimony was simple, direct, and believable. It held up fine under my brief cross-examination. Mr. B insisted on taking the stand in his own defense and all but convicted himself with his own words. The jury obviously liked the guy, though, and they stayed out for quite a while deliberating, or maybe eating a leisurely lunch. They finally did the only thing they could do; they came back with a conviction.

The judge was in a bad mood at sentencing. The old guy was charming, but he had screwed up the calendar. Even worse, the judge couldn't shake the feeling that the defendant had somehow mocked the system and made the court look a little foolish, petty, and harsh.

"I am sentencing you to eighteen months, to be served *consecutively* to the sentence you are currently serving." The dreaded word *consecutively* could make a prisoner's heart sink. It meant he would have to serve every day of his present sentence before beginning the new one being imposed. Mr. B looked up at the judge and smiled. The judge mustered a scowl and went on with, "I'm not sure, but I have the feeling that I'm doing exactly what you want me to do," and for once he hit it right.

I felt a little sad—not crushed, as I would have felt when I started the PD job, but still sad for Mr. B. He had family, but no one showed up during the trial or at sentencing. They probably had a good reason for staying away. Who knows, he may have been a lousy father, husband, brother, whatever, but it still seemed a shame to be alone and going off to prison again at an age when he should have been with family or hanging out with his old buddies, telling stories and spending his social security checks.

The prosecutor came over to me after sentencing and said, "You know, at one point in the trial, I caught him looking at you like you were his son, and was so proud of you."

Just about the same time Mr. B approached, shook my hand, and patted me on the back just before the sheriff's deputies put the handcuffs on him and led him out. He was happy. A rare satisfied customer of the public defender. He'd gotten what he wanted, another eighteen months as a guest of the state of New Jersey—another year and a half with a roof over his head before he would have to confront the mean streets one more time.

MICHAEL J. CARROLL
STAFF ATTORNEY
COMMUNITY LEGAL SERVICES, INC.
PHILADELPHIA, PENNSYLVANIA

More Than She Could Stomach

THE NEWLY ELECTED SHERIFF OF A CENTRAL INDIANA COUNTY was riding his teenage son's bicycle through the neighborhood one evening when one of the pedals came off. In the resulting crash, the sheriff's mouth got smashed up pretty badly, requiring some restorative dental work and resulting in a minor scar on his upper lip, which he claimed he was so self-conscious about he just had to grow a less-than-flattering mustache.

The sheriff sued.

The manufacturers of the bicycle and the pedal assembly quickly settled, but my client—the local power tool/lawn-care-equipment/hardware/sporting-goods store—wouldn't. So the sheriff's case went to trial. As it turned out, the "first chair" at trial for each side was occupied by junior lawyers, new to the bar—one of them me. Each of us was trying a jury case for the first time, and doing so under the watchful eyes of a junior partner charged with the responsibility of making sure nothing went too terribly wrong on his side of the courtroom.

This was the presiding judge's last trial. In the recent election—the one in which the sheriff had been elected—the judge had been defeated. While not the easiest jurist to satisfy in the best of times, he didn't seem to let his obvious disappointment noticeably affect his performance. Both rookie trial lawyers managed to pick a jury, make opening statements, and complete the presentation of evidence with minimal assistance from our more senior colleagues and without suffering any major mishaps. Plaintiff's closing argument was also delivered without incident. However, approximately three minutes into my first-ever closing argument to a jury, one of the jurors stood up and walked out of the courtroom without saying a word to anyone.

The silence seemed to go on forever as I frantically reviewed my options to deal with a situation for which neither my formal legal education nor my limited litigation experience had prepared me. Just as I had decided to ask the judge how *he* wanted to proceed, my mentor, seated back at the defense table from which I had arisen to go to the podium to address the jury, cheerfully offered this observation: "Personally, Your Honor, I didn't think he was that bad!"

After order was restored in the court, the departed juror was located and explained that her court-supplied lunch had disagreed with her to the point that she didn't think it was a good idea to delay her departure from the courtroom long enough to offer an explanation. The parties then agreed to have the case decided by the eleven jurors still in the box, and my first defense verdict was returned in reasonably short order.

I'm not sure whether the sheriff was still upset about his loss at trial when a few months later he beat up the jail inmates who had drawn some unflattering pictures of his wife, but that's another story. . . .

W. C. BLANTON
OPPENHEIMER WOLFF & DONNELLY LLP
MINNEAPOLIS, MINNESOTA

Miami Vice

THE RAUCOUS 1994 MAYORAL ELECTION IN THE MOSTLY IN-
dustrial and predominantly Cuban town of Hialeah, sprawling next to
Miami, was dramatically close. My client had lost the election by just over
one hundred votes. The incumbent ("Raul"), rich and flamboyant, had
gathered an unprecedented number of absentee ballots. While he was
powerful and popular, he had also been the target of a number of federal
corruption indictments and trials, and had been expected to lose.

Cubans are a wonderfully warm and colorful people. They have a natural love for politics and they love to talk, mostly with their hands and frequently with little cups of coffee ("cafesitos"), which contain nuclear
quantities of caffeine. This makes them more excited and talk faster. Consequently, there is a passionate quality to Cuban politics. Like all politics,
it is occasionally corrupt.

Rumors swirled in coffee shops all over the city. Stories of secret
squads of city employees procuring forged absentee ballots percolated
around dinner tables and sidewalks. After investigation, the charges took
the form of a civil lawsuit challenging the election.

Florida law intentionally makes it difficult to void an election. Clear
proof of a tainted process is required. The judge both tries the facts and
interprets the law in this type of proceeding. As was my luck, the judge was
a Democrat, like the mayor. The judge was also up for election, a fact that
did not go unnoticed by the mayor's political machine.

It turned out that a number of absentee ballots had been collected at
licensed Adult Congregate Living Facilities ("flophouses"), where drug-
gies, drunks, the sick, the weak, and the desperate lived. When I deposed
these citizens, they could not identify their signatures. Dozens of phony
ballots had come from nursing homes, signed by *viejas* (old ladies), some
of whom identified Roosevelt as the current president. Other ballots came

from voters who lived in other cities and states but had declared themselves Hialeah citizens only for election day, which of course was unlawful. Many were just plain forgeries, poorly done.

Months passed as I took hundreds of depositions of voters and campaign workers, many invoking their Fifth Amendment right against self-incrimination. The emotional level rose geometrically as the trial neared. Threats regularly rolled into our office with the deponents. One day a sweet elderly couple started suddenly cursing at me and shouting "Viva Raul!" to avoid my questions.

During the trial each side sat behind their favorite lawyer, making threatening faces and pornographic gestures (out of sight of the judge) at the other camp. Each day I was greeted with *abrazos* (hugs) and trial advice as I entered the courtroom. Each evening as I left, a good day of examination would be enthusiastically rewarded. A bad day would be forgiven by accusing the witness of *mentiras* (lies).

I could tell by the mayor's face, however, that we were winning.

One early morning close to the end of trial, my wife called me to view our front lawn. Someone had left a Santeria curse. The Santeria religion is a Cuban mix of Catholicism and voodoo, revolving around a saint called Babaloo. Curses and antidotes are available for just about any occasion. In our case, we were hexed with bright blue eggs, feathers, coins, and other strange things.

When I came to court, I reported the curse to my client, who sought the advice of someone else more expert. One woman screamed out "Dios, Dios," which unsettled me. To make matters worse, an ugly woman oddly dressed in pure black kept staring at me. I could feel the searing glare on the back of my neck. My client identified her as a priestess employed by the opposition. But the next day, the final day of closing arguments, a woman dressed all in white was sitting on our side of the courtroom. My client seemed pleased and relaxed and the trial ended.

The judge announced by written order that he had marshaled up the facts and the law persuasively enough to void the election. I was declared a hero by the Cuban forces of good and El Diablo (the Devil) by the other guys.

A new election was called, which was more vicious than the first one. Even more absentee ballots were cast.

My client lost, by even more votes than the first time.

It was strongly suggested to me that I not be seen in Hialeah anytime soon.

THOMAS R. SPENCER, JR.
SPENCER & KLEIN, P.A.
MIAMI, FLORIDA

Juvenile Justice

I WAS A PROSECUTOR IN MEMPHIS, BRAND-NEW TO THE JOB. IT was arraignment day, that part of the week when all those indicted the week before would come before the court for their initial appearance. Those who pled guilty would be held over for sentencing. Those who pled not guilty would be held over for trial. The morning was a parade of defendants, some with their defense lawyers, others who would show up alone and need the court to appoint counsel for them. The rest of the courtroom was filled with the prosecutors, patiently waiting for their cases to be called.

One of the more senior prosecutors sat in the row in front of me, absentmindedly looking at his case files. The clerk called out the first case of the day, one of his cases. The charge was illegally tending a moonshine still. As the name of the defendant was called, a young boy, no more than twelve years old, rose and walked slowly toward the judge's bench. The prosecutor looked at the boy, then down again at his file. Sure enough, a mistake had been made. The indictment returned by the grand jury was against a twelve-year-old boy. This was not juvenile court, mind you, but the federal court in Memphis. To make matters worse, the judge that day was the most senior member of the bench, well over seventy, and known with justification as a hanging judge.

At that moment the prosecutor was uncertain as to who was going to be "hanged," the twelve-year-old defendant or him for having indicted this child who was at that moment standing before the podium in the front of the courtroom waiting for the proceedings to begin.

The prosecutor slowly rose and walked toward the front of the courtroom, placing himself directly beside the young boy and bracing himself as best he could against the tirade that he was certain was about to erupt from the judge.

The boy was so small, however, that his head did not reach above the podium. So as he and the prosecutor stood there side by side, the judge searched down across the space in front of him, and seeing no one but the prosecutor, went through the formalities of calling out the defendant's name and inquiring if anyone by that name was in the courtroom. Normal procedure for the nonappearance of an indicted defendant is the issuance of a warrant of arrest and what amounts to an all-points bulletin to the police to arrest and jail on sight.

The child, not knowing what was going on, looked from side to side, and then hearing his name called out by the judge, was about to answer when the prosecutor spoke to the court.

Without actually mentioning that the defendant was standing right there beside him, the prosecutor notified the court in a little speech about the interests of justice and "a closer look at the facts and circumstances surrounding this case" that the United States had decided the case was not worthy of prosecution and would therefore be dismissed. With the court's permission, of course, the prosecutor added. The busy judge, not seeing a defendant standing before him in the first place, waved the prosecutor away so he could tend to the next in a long line of cases waiting to be heard that day.

And then, as though he were showing a Boy Scout on a civics outing around the courtroom, the prosecutor nonchalantly placed his hand on the young defendant's shoulder and walked him away from the podium and out of the courtroom.

It was a masterly performance by a lawyer.

LARRY E. PARRISH
PARRISH, SHAW & BRANDON
MEMPHIS, TENNESSEE

Don't Try This at Home

I WAS WORKING ON A LARGE AND COMPLEX CORPORATE AC-quisition that was supposed to close in time for me to spend a summer vacation with my wife and new baby on the Scottish island of Skye. Unfortunately, the timetable slipped and the client was reluctant to release me for something as trivial as a family vacation. We hammered out a compromise. Until the deal closed, I would stay in London Monday through Friday to attend the drafting meetings and would be released to spend the weekends with the family. Fine in theory.

The full resources of my law firm were devoted to making the travel arrangements for my first weekend furlough. The best they could come up with was an overnight sleeper train from London to Inverness, a rental car from the aptly named Sharp's Reliable Wrecks, and the ferry from the mainland to Skye.

I emerged, blinking, at 7:30 P.M. on the Friday from a marathon thirty-six-hour meeting and headed straight for the train station. I noticed that one of my shoes had fallen apart, but I didn't have time to go home and change. I figured I'd buy new shoes during the weekend.

On the train, instead of sleeping, I worked on the deal documents. On arrival at Inverness, I picked up my rental car and, for £7.50, made the best investment of my career. I bought a full collision damage waiver.

I enjoyed my drive through the splendid Highland scenery—at least till I fell asleep. I don't remember much about the impact though I clearly recall the surprised look on the face of the driver of the other car as I careered into her on a mountain bend. Fortunately, though both cars were totally wrecked, there were no injuries.

One of the witnesses pulled me through my car window and observed that, when I braced myself for the impact, I had stepped down so hard that I broke my shoe. I didn't want people to think I was the kind of guy who walks around in broken shoes so I readily agreed to this assessment.

All the witnesses went to the local police station to make statements. As the obviously guilty party, I asked if I could avail myself of the right to telephone a lawyer. The police were happy to oblige, so I called one of the lawyers working on the deal and discussed amendments to the deal documents until it was my turn to confess.

We closed the deal a year later and I found myself in Chicago with the lawyer I had called from the police station. He agreed to rent a car with me for the duration of our visit.

But for some reason he insisted on doing all the driving.

IAN FAGELSON
WARNER CRANSTON
LONDON, ENGLAND

Coffee, Tea, or Me

SEVERAL YEARS AGO I REPRESENTED A CLIENT WHO WAS BUY-ing a business directly from the seller; no lawyers were involved in the negotiations. When an agreement in principle was reached, and hands were shaken, the buyer and the seller called their lawyers so a meeting could be arranged to review the details of the deal. The meeting was scheduled to take place in my law office.

Promptly at 8:30 A.M. on the day of the meeting, the seller's lawyer and his client arrived and were shown into a conference room. My client arrived a few minutes before I did, so that when I walked into the room everyone else was already seated.

Sooner or later, every working woman who is not a secretary is going to be assumed to be one. So I shouldn't have been surprised when no sooner had I walked into the room than the seller's lawyer demanded coffee. Our firm's coffee service didn't begin until 9:00 A.M., so I left and went to the kitchen myself. When I returned to the conference with a tray holding a coffee carafe and cups, the lawyer, with what I took to be clear annoyance at my incompetence, asked for artificial sweetener. I smiled pleasantly at him, told him that I was very sorry for the oversight, and would go right back to the kitchen. As I turned to leave I winked at my client, signaling that he shouldn't let on who I was.

I returned with his sweetener, grabbed one of the legal pads that were stacked in the center of the table, and took the seat next to my client.

"Shall we begin?" I asked.

The seller's lawyer, particularly slow on the uptake, looked at his watch in further annoyance, obviously wondering where *Mr.* Aftab was, and why "his" secretary would start a meeting without him. Then it hit him. I watched his jaw drop.

The lawyer said nothing. In fact, he remained silent through the first part of our discussions, in which his client conceded two of the three important points my clients wanted included in the contract of sale. Eventually, he restored the wind in his sails, but by then the details of the deal had already been completed.

My client asked if I wouldn't mind arriving a few minutes late for all our meetings.

PARRY AFTAB
AFTAB & SAVITT, P.C.
SPRINGFIELD, NEW JERSEY

More Days in the Life . . .

Hats Off

When I began practicing criminal law eighteen years ago there were not a lot of women in the field. The way I remember it, those of us who did appear as defense lawyers were generally short, mouthy, and Jewish. As someone who is generally short, mouthy, and Jewish myself, I had to make a special effort to separate myself from the Levys, Rosenbergs, and Finkelsteins. I took to wearing hats and carrying a very bright red rubber briefcase. Picture two red bath mats sewn together with a zipper and you've got the picture. My hats distinguished me—well, from the other ladies, at least. The judges got the picture: Rosenthal was the one in the hat.

> JUDGE: "Well, if it isn't Ms. Rosenthal, and her ever-present hat."
> ME: "Good morning, Judge."
> JUDGE: "Why the hat, Ms. Rosenthal? Did they give you a hats course in law school?"
> ME: "Would you like me to remove it, Your Honor?"
> JUDGE: "No. I've seen you without your hat. You can leave it on."

It's important to let the judge think he's being clever.

Feel-Good Cases

I'll call her Mary (not her real name). She was about thirty-five years old when I met her, although she looked fifty. Skinny frame, few teeth. I was assigned by the court to represent her. She had served time for stabbing a guy to death in a drunken stupor. Anyway, when I got the case, the Department of Social Services had swooped in and taken her newborn baby from her at the hospital on the theory of imminent danger. She had killed before, she had been a drunk. She could do it again.

So, after eighteen hours of labor, and less than a full day with her new baby, she was visited by three proctors from the Department of Social Services, who proceeded to take her baby from her. If you can imagine a more vulnerable moment in a woman's life, share it with me, because I can't.

At our first meeting, I was struck by her tiny size. She couldn't have weighed more than 100 pounds. But she was tough. Apparently, she had survived prison with a mouth and an attitude that kept the more dangerous inmates at bay. In any event, she told me all about the murder, her time in prison, and the fact that she was trying to start a new life, complete with baby and sobriety. She had been sober for the two years she had been out of jail. Apparently, DSS had never even bothered to check out her new life.

When we finally appeared before the family court judge, I managed to prove that Mary had complied with all of her parole conditions, had maintained sobriety, and had every intention of performing her motherhood duties for her newborn infant. The judge was furious with the DSS and immediately dismissed the petition, ordering the return of the infant. For years after, I would run into Mary and she would show me pictures of her girl. As far as I know, she and her daughter are still doing well.

I will always remember this case because of the utter cruelty of ripping an infant from a mother's arms on rumor and unfounded accusations.

As Simple as Black and White

I had been court-appointed to defend the accused in a felony criminal case. My client (David) had been charged with assaulting another man (Paul).

David had met Paul because Paul worked in the same diner as David's then girlfriend (Donna). It seems that David had come into the diner and begun an argument with Donna, and when he threatened to shoot her, she called the cops. David was charged with harassment and attempted assault. At his court arraignment a few days latter, Paul accompanied Donna. Bystanders later remembered David glaring at Paul as Donna's charges were read out to him. Three days later, as Paul was walking home alone, he was hit from behind with a heavy metal object. At the hospital he was asked whether he could identify his attacker, and he named David.

I get the case. I have never tried a felony. I try to plea-bargain. The DA offers a plea to one assault count and reduced prison time. David says no deal. He's innocent. He didn't do it. On the morning of trial the DA offers a better deal. A plea to one count and probation. David still says no way. It's then that I realize that he probably *is* innocent. Why else would he turn down an offer of probation?

Now I'm scared. What if I botch this? Innocent people do get convicted. What if I take this case to trial and do my best and David still gets convicted? What then? This is no time for hand-wringing, I tell myself. We select a jury and the trial begins. Paul is the prosecution's first witness. The direct examination doesn't take long.

Soon enough, the DA asks Paul the ultimate question: Do you see your attacker in the courtroom?

Paul looks around, first at the judge (he's white), then at the DA (white, also), then at the jury (all white), then at me (not even the right sex), and then at David (the only black person in the entire courtroom). He stares at David, who by the way has no alibi for the time of the attack, other than that he was home, alone, and asleep. Then he says no, he can't identify his attacker. (I thought I had died and gone to heaven.) Then the DA starts to ask the question again, suggesting that maybe if Paul were to study the defendant more closely . . . I rise to my feet and object. The judge sustains the objection. He calls a recess.

After court resumes, the DA rises to address the judge. He moves to dismiss. Motion granted.

The local paper writes an editorial about how awful it was that this poor guy had to go through all this and be saddled with the expense of a lawyer. Of course, I was assigned counsel, so it didn't cost him a cent. Still, if Paul had been a little less honest, David would probably have gone to jail.

Don't Touch That

My client was charged with shoplifting. The item in question was a large pepperoni sausage, which when he was apprehended he had stuffed in the front of his pants. It reminded me of the old Mae West line, "Is that a pis-

tol you've hidden in your pocket, honey, or are you just glad to see me?"
We plea-bargained. Case concluded.

I had a pepperoni sent to the DA as a token of my appreciation. (I
didn't tell him it was a new one.)

KATE ROSENTHAL, ESQUIRE
SYRACUSE, NEW YORK

The Immigration Officer

M R. OBINSKI IS AN ELDERLY GENTLEMAN OF POLISH ORIGIN. He is tall, slender, and erect, and has a serious demeanor. One day he appears in my office with a very nice elderly lady, Mrs. Warren. She is petite and attractive and her face reveals the successor to that of a once beautiful young woman. She has a disarming charm and an ever-present smile that elicits a like response from me whenever she speaks to me.

Mrs. Warren is a U.S. citizen and wants to hire me to help her file a petition for permanent residency for Mr. Obinski, her newlywed husband.

The pair met while they both were Polish university students in France, just prior to the outbreak of World War II. They fell in love, then planned to marry, but their plans were dashed when the war started. Poland was overrun so quickly by Nazi Germany that it was impossible for them to return to Poland in time to lend any support to the Polish government's futile war effort. Seven months later, France was also defeated by the German war machine, so they, and other Polish student expatriates, joined and became active in the French underground for the balance of the war.

As a result of wartime exigencies, they were separated and never saw each other again—until recently. During these years apart, both of them married other people and went on with their lives. Mrs. Warren married an American civilian government employee who had been assigned to postwar France. They eventually settled in the United States, where she became a citizen. Recently, Mr. Warren passed away.

Mr. Obinski married a Frenchwoman after the war, continued to live in France, and eventually became a French citizen. His wife also died some years ago, and he continued to live in France and remained active in certain Polish underground veteran affairs. While attending a meeting of his underground World War II veteran colleagues in the United States, he reencountered Mrs. Warren, the erstwhile young woman with whom he had been in love in 1939—almost a half century ago. They rekindled their courtship and got married, and now they appear in my office so that Mrs. Warren can file a petition for permanent residency for Mr. Obinski.

The entire time they are telling me this story, alternating from one to the other, they are holding hands. Mr. Obinski never displays any emotion or any other sense of informality, while Mrs. Warren cannot mask her affection and joy at being reunited with him. However, when he speaks about Mrs. Warren and looks at her, the devotion he feels for her is quite apparent.

I filed the papers for them. At that time, the procedure provided for aliens to receive permanent residency in the United States without having to return to their home country, so long as they did not depart the United States after the petition was filed.

One day, several weeks later, Mr. Obinski came to my office and told me he must return to France, even if it would jeopardize his permanent residency application status. I told him that if he did go, at his age and given the length of time it would then take to process his papers at the U.S. consulate in Paris, his ability to return to the United States would be very chancy indeed. At best, he would risk a substantial delay in being able to return.

Mr. Obinski quietly and sadly said that he had to go. I was stunned and pressed him for a reason for his departure, since it was obvious that he and Mrs. Warren were absolutely in love with each other. It was as if they were reincarnated college students! After some pressing, he told me that he was attending a reunion of his Polish underground colleagues, who were celebrating the fortieth anniversary of the end of World War II. He told me that some of the bravest and most loyal men and women he had ever met were members of this unit. They all had sworn that they would always attend their meetings in honor of their colleagues who died during the war and those who died thereafter.

I took a few moments to assimilate what he was saying, then realized that this man must have agonized over the choice between honoring the commitment he had made to his wartime colleagues and restarting his life with his long-lost love. After a brief silence, I told him I understood his conflict and his choice, but I could not guarantee that the Immigration Service would allow him to obtain his permanent residency in the United States, also known as his adjustment of status.

As the date for the interview for adjustment of status neared, I sent my routine letter to the clients asking them to meet me at the Immigration Service and to bring certain documents needed to complete the process. Recognizing that I had a very special case, I sent a long letter to the Immigration Office that I hoped would find its way into my clients' file. This letter explained the compelling circumstances surrounding Mr. Obinski's decision to leave the United States while his application for legal permanent residence status was pending and requested a favorable exercise of discretion for these extraordinary clients.

On the day of the interview, I met with Mr. Obinski and Mrs. Warren and spoke briefly with them about some of the documents they brought concerning employment, pension income, and so on. I asked them if they were ready. I did not mention the trip outside the United States, but it was apparent that all of us were aware of the risk they were running. All the while Mrs. Warren held tightly to Mr. Obinski's arm.

While we were waiting to be called into the interview, one of my immigration colleagues came out from an interview session. I told him about my client's situation and asked for his advice. In his words, the case was "a loser" and my client's petition "was going to be denied." Great news—just what I needed to hear right before the interview.

Our turn came and we were called into the meeting room. We sat in front of a stone-faced, barrel-chested INS officer who did not greet us in any way. He just silently reviewed the file and did not hide his annoyance at having to deal with so many documents. Among the documents he reviewed was a report prepared by the immigration inspector who had interviewed Mr. Obinski at the airport in Atlanta upon his recent reentry to the United States. A frown crossed our officer's face as he perused that report as well as Mr. Obinski's passport.

The officer then went on a harangue about how he should not grant this application and how he could not believe that Mr. Obinski had been able to reenter the United States. Addressing Mr. Obinski, the officer asked rhetorically what could have been on my client's mind when he departed the United States without advance permission. The officer then intimated that Mr. Obinski must have committed fraud at the border in order to gain reentry to the United States. What really bothered me was the way in which the officer kept referring to my client, a war hero, by his first name, Peter, in a demeaning and disparaging manner.

During these interviews lawyers are not permitted to speak except at the request of the examining officer, but I could not stand it any longer.

When the officer was about to deny the requests, I asked him—in almost a whisper—if he had seen my letter. The officer complained while fumbling through the voluminous file and grumbled that my letter would make no difference to him—and then he found it. He read the letter silently, both pages. The officer sat silently staring at the file for a few moments and then looked up at Mr. Obinski and said in a soft and different voice, "I'm approving the petition." He said nothing further to any of us, but when the interview was over he stood up and offered his handshake to Mr. Obinski.

When we walked back out into the reception room, I congratulated my clients and they hugged and kissed. Mr. Obinski pressed his wife's head to his chest in a gesture that emanated from another time and another place. We took the elevator down to the street level without saying a word to one another. Once outside, we exchanged our departure civilities and Mrs. Warren gave me a tearful hug. We then went off in two different directions.

When I reached the corner I turned and looked at my clients as they were walking slowly away from me. They were holding hands, like two young teenagers, and she had her head pressed against his arm. I never saw or heard from them again.

RAMON CARRION
ATTORNEY AT LAW
CLEARWATER, FLORIDA

Disorder in the Court V

QUESTION: Tell us your full name, please.
ANSWER: Mine?
QUESTION: Yes, sir.
ANSWER: 555-2733.
QUESTION: Mr. Daniels, do you have any problem hearing me?
ANSWER: Not really.
QUESTION: Where do you live?
ANSWER: Pardon?

QUESTION: Are you restricted in some way from having your
    third finger shot off?
ANSWER: Yeah, a little.
QUESTION: What could you do before the accident that you can't
    do now?
ANSWER: Wear a ring on it.

QUESTION: Do you know whether or not your daughter has
    ever been involved in voodoo or the occult?
ANSWER: No, I don't know if she practices.
QUESTION: Do you know if she buys any publications on
    voodoo?
ANSWER: We both do.
QUESTION: Voodoo?
ANSWER: We do.
QUESTION: You do?
ANSWER: Yes, voodoo.

*   *   *

QUESTION: Did you blow your horn or anything?

ANSWER: After the accident?

QUESTION: Before the accident?

ANSWER: Sure, I played for ten years. I went to school for it and everything.

QUESTION: And all the items included in that photograph—were they present at the time that photograph was taken?

ANSWER: Yes, sir.

QUESTION: Were you conceived prior to your father leaving, or were you conceived after your father left?

MR. HARTER: I don't know if that works.

QUESTION: Can you describe that individual?

ANSWER: He was about medium height and had a beard.

QUESTION: Was this a male or a female?

QUESTION: Have you ever tried to commit suicide?

ANSWER: Yes, sir.

QUESTION: Were you ever successful?

ANSWER: No, sir.

QUESTION: Doctor, how many autopsies have you performed on dead people?

ANSWER: All my autopsies have been on dead people.

The Divorce

THE WIFE WAS FROM A WEST VIRGINIA COALMINER'S FAMILY of ten children and had left high school before graduating. The husband had been born in Eastern Europe, emigrating to the United States as a young adult and working more or less steadily as a carpenter. The husband maintained his Old World habits. He neglected his wife and kids. When he was in a bad mood, he would physically abuse her.

When she consulted me about a divorce, we agreed I would get started with the little bit of money she had. The balance of my fee would be paid when she received her share of the marital property.

Equitable distribution of the marital property is supposed to result in a fair division of marital assets, without regard to whose fault caused the divorce, and both parties should come away with their fair share of the pot. In our case the husband put his position succinctly to his wife:

"You don't want to sleep with me, you can go fuck yourself. Nothing. You get nothing from me."

Ordinarily when the husband has to pay a lawyer who advises him that the law doesn't support this view, he is willing to settle. But in this case, our husband met up with a lawyer who was only too glad to get a steady supply of fee money in return for not disabusing the client of his quaint notion. This meant that every step of the way was opposed, from temporary support of the wife, up to and including who was to remain in the marital home while the lawsuit proceeded. The court had to be asked to intervene in these matters, even before it would be asked to hear the main part of the action, which was the divorce and the distribution of the property.

Each time an application to the court was made, all of us had to be present in court. Judges regularly require this to encourage the parties to settle their differences, and thus save the court from making decisions that might not be as satisfactory to either or both of them. In general, lawyers know that judges are much too busy to manage the day-to-day affairs of clients, so they dutifully take the opportunity when both parties are present and waiting to go before a judge to try to negotiate a settlement.

But again, in our case, the husband's obstinacy was not relieved by his counsel, and we wound up having to put the court to the trouble of hearing the messy details, which made all of us very unpopular with the judge.

The proceedings lasted three long years. Not only was there a trial, after which both were awarded a divorce, but we had a second trial on the distribution of the marital assets. After this, the judge announced that he would order the sale of the marital home and real estate. I understood then that I somehow had to find a way to settle and avoid such a sale, sure to be disastrous for my client, since her husband could easily find someone to buy it for him at a ridiculously low price, which would eliminate any profit to be divided, equitably or not.

By this time, seeing the stream of fees coming to an end, even the other lawyer was ready to settle. He got his client to offer mine a sum of money plus title to another parcel of real property with a house on it. I thought it was as good as we were likely to get. The settlement was read into the record, the judge congratulated us on finally achieving an accord, and he went on to the next case. It was time for us to leave the courtroom for good.

My client walked beside me on the way out, but instead of relief it was fury I saw on her face. There would be no more dressing up to attend proceedings in an impressive and dignified setting, no more conferences between counsel and the judge, after which she would have to be consulted. By this time we had reached the head of the stairway leading to the ground floor, a grand staircase with about thirty marble steps. Her anger escalated into a kind of madness, causing her to make rapid, jerky movements of her body, one of which sent her off balance just as she started descending the steps, within easy reach of the handrail.

I watched her go down, realize how to save herself, then decide not to, and tumble all the rest of the way. She was a tall, bony woman, with no fat to buffer the fall. But she was transfused with an emotion that gave her superhuman powers, evidently, because after at last reaching the bottom, before horrified lookers-on, she picked herself up, shrugged off their offers of concern, and, taking long strides, slowly left the building.

I never saw her again after that day.

ISABELLE RAWICH
ATTORNEY AT LAW
SOUTH FALLSBURG, NEW YORK

Dog Days

I HAD SPENT SEVEN YEARS IN THE UNITED STATES ATTORNEY'S office, then gone into private practice, first in a smaller law firm, then in a larger one whose main client base was, and is, corporate America.

I had been there only a few weeks as a junior partner, when one of the senior partners asked me to meet with him. Partners in most law firms spend at least some of their professional time looking for new clients. This sort of activity often consists of preparing papers on legal topics of interest to potential corporate clients, or giving speeches to business roundtables and the like. Sometimes a luncheon or dinner is arranged at a nice restaurant to meet and greet corporate executives who could steer some legal business the firm's way. Nice, scholarly, fancy get-togethers—all designed to showcase the abilities of the lawyers and their firm. So when I was asked to meet with one of the firm's most senior partners, I must confess I figured that he was about to involve me in one or another of these activities. But that's not exactly how our conversation began.

"You a hunter?" he asked.

I shrugged my shoulders, like isn't everybody a hunter? Then, while nonchalantly examining the crease in my trousers, I blew a short puff of air through my lips. You know, in order to show him—Can I hunt? Are you kidding? I was born hunting. (Fact is, I had seen *Wild Kingdom* on TV as a kid, and I could remember the host of the weekly program, dressed in bush khakis, his thin white mustache and angular face that of the great white hunter. Each Saturday he and his guests would stalk and kill gazelle or some other exotic animal. At least that was the way I remembered it. And that—needless to say—was the full and complete extent of my "hunting" experience.)

Frankly, what I had expected to hear from this senior partner was his interest in collaborating with me on a law review article on some cutting-

edge legal issue, or maybe he was going to invite me to attend some business dinner at one of the finer French restaurants. But no. He wanted to
know if I could hunt. Now, I'm a smart fellow. This was business genera-
tion. Business development. There was going to be a hunting party. Client
types would be there. You know, guys from big corporations, with pot-
bellies, who eat big meals, drink gin and fine wine—and send big business
to big law firms. "No, I don't hunt" as an answer would mean that this
partner would probably say, too bad, that's a shame. Then he would reach
for his intercom and ask his secretary to call some other junior partner.
One who could hunt. And there would go my chance for new business.

"Hunting," I repeated, not yet fully able to make eye contact with him
on this topic. "Great sport," I mumbled. I think I may have repeated this
last phrase a time or two.

"Good," the senior partner said, then gave me directions to the hunting lodge. Dinner Thursday night starts at 8:00 P.M., hunting Friday morning at 4:45 A.M. That's what he said: *4:45* A.M. I nodded agreeably. Hey, no
problem. I do all my hunting at 4:45 in the morning. I felt like hitching up
my pants, maybe spitting some tobacco juice down past my tasseled loafer
onto his expensive Persian carpet. He then laid out the rest of the schedule. Dinner would be followed by brandy and a few hours of social
schmoozing. Nothing directly about business, but the corporate bigwigs
invited to the hunting party knew why they were there, too. Then after
about two or three hours of sleep, goose hunting. After the hunt there
would be lunch—a big lunch—then more hunting. Dinner the second
night, of course. More late-night brandy. The schmooze fest would then
continue. No real sleep again, followed by the second day's goose hunting.

"Great, sounds great," I said. (I was still repeating myself at this point.
If he noticed, he didn't let on.) Then I rose and headed for the door.

I didn't go back to my office. Nope, I went straight for the elevators,
down to the lobby, and out to the street, where the first cab I caught drove
me to a sports outfitter. In less than twenty minutes—and $1,500 later—I
had acquired every article of attire any goose hunter would ever need.
Boots, thermal-lined pants, a camouflage hat—you name it. The young
salesman who waited on me couldn't believe his good fortune, making his
sales quota before lunch. Then, with the salesman's help, I located a gun
range where I booked two quick lessons on how to operate and fire a
twelve-gauge shotgun. (That's what the salesman told me I'd be using on
the goose hunt.)

A few days later there I was, in a goose blind at the water's edge, freezing my butt off along with my senior partner and several prospective client types. Now, for those of you who've never seen a hunting blind, it's a large rectangular boxlike structure where the hunters and their guide sit, usually uncomfortably, waiting patiently as the guide, who from time to time honks out simulated goose sounds on a wooden quacker, tries to lure a flock of geese overhead for execution.

The first day's hunting was relatively uneventful. The kickoff dinner the night before had been pleasant enough, although I was a bit tired from the late night's eating and drinking. There was one mildly embarrassing moment in the blind that day when all of us fired at some geese, and only one dropped. "Hey, good shot," my senior partner said to the corporate president who had been placed next to him. "Good shot."

"Better than good," the corporate president said in return. "A great shot," he said as he cracked open his shotgun to show that he hadn't even fired. (It seemed that my partner had instructed the hunting guide to stand behind this guest and fire his own shotgun at the overhead geese to ensure a kill. Credited to the corporate executive, of course.) I must hand it to my partner. Without missing a beat, he let out a belly laugh and made the most wonderful joke out of this embarrassing situation. Within seconds, all of us in the goose blind were laughing. God bless corporate America.

All in all, I think I did pretty well. I yukked it up with the boys, listened to and laughed at the off-color jokes, held my liquor pretty well, and nodded sagely on those few occasions when my partner touted the attributes of our firm. That is, I think I did pretty well, until the morning of the second day's hunting. If it hadn't been for that damned dog . . .

The second's day's shoot was in a different hunting blind. This one was not at the water's edge but in a field on a farm. The blind we used on the second day was more like a reinforced pit in the ground. There was a long bench for the hunters to sit on. All of our shotguns were lined up in front of us, resting against the front retaining wall. There was camouflage brush over our heads. There was also no breeze, no airflow, just all of us, the guide included, sitting in this airless pit, waiting. There was another inhabitant of this blind. Lying right at my feet was the guide's hunting dog, seemingly asleep, waiting for birds to fall from the sky for him to fetch.

I'll admit I wasn't feeling too well that morning. I'd had two late nights, a lot of heavy food. And, yes, probably too much booze. I was tired—really tired. And I had a major headache. (Yeah, okay, I was hung over.)

Anyway, here I am in the blind. My partner lights up a cigar. The guy seated next to me, who looks half dead himself, stifles a cough. The guide, who is now crouching down at my knees, next to his dog, starts blowing on his honker, sending out shrill, blaring goose sounds, which reverberate off the walls of this airless tomb we are all sitting in. And then the dog farts.

Now, I don't know what the guide had fed that dog the night before. But whatever it was, it had chemically transformed itself into Desert Storm–grade, germ-warfare poison gas. It was awful. It made rotten eggs smell like freshly cut roses. But I held on. I stopped all forms of breathing, but I held on. But the dog—still lying there as though it was asleep—wasn't satisfied with just one fart. Oh no, it had to fart again. And then again, and again. I couldn't breathe.

I looked quickly over to my senior partner. He seemed comfortable enough, sitting at the far end of the bench, smoking his cigar. Smoking his cigar! Of course, I thought to myself. He knows, he's done this before. That's why the cigar. He's masking the dog's noxious fumes with fumes of his own. All the while the guide—himself seemingly oblivious to the dog's putrid vapors—has continued quacking on his goose honker with a determination I was finding intolerable. For God's sake, didn't anyone down here realize that we were dying? Finally, I spoke.

"Dog's gotta go," I said to the guide.

At first he ignored me, or he simply hadn't heard what I had said, the way he was furiously honking at geese that were nowhere in sight. I waited patiently (about a nanosecond), then repeated myself, this time with real feeling, if not desperation.

"Dog's gotta go."

The guide momentarily stopped his honking. He looked briefly in my direction. When our eyes met I could see that this man was not what you'd call a bright light. He was probably a wonderful hunter, but human discourse, the give-and-take of polite, civilized conversation (like "dog's gotta go"), was not something with which he was familiar.

"Can't," the guide finally said as he returned to his honker.

I touched his shoulder. Remember, he was kneeling at my feet at the time. He turned back to me again, this time with clear impatience on his face.

"Throw the dog out of the blind," I said to him.

He stared at me. His eyes blinked a time or two. Throw the dog out of the blind, he seemed to be thinking. Throw the dog out of the blind. What, are you crazy? Throw the dog out of the blind in the middle of goose hunt-ing? While we're all down here in this unlimed outhouse, camouflaged, waiting patiently for unsuspecting geese to fly over. At any minute, you fool!

Now to his credit, the guide didn't say any of this to me. But he was clearly thinking it. I could tell by his blinks. What he said was "Can't," then he turned and went back to honking. No sooner had he turned when the dog farted again. This one was a beaut. A real beaut. It was rank. Foul. Loathsome. It was all I could take.

I reached over to where my shotgun was stacked, right there in front of me, to the side of the crouching, honking guide. I took the shotgun. The guide turned and looked at me.

"Throw the dog out of the blind," I repeated. The guide gave me this thin little smile—you know, like to say, Oh really? And what are you go-ing to do if I don't, you little city-boy ass-wipe lawyer. He didn't say any of this. He simply gave me his little smile. Civilized conversation was not his strong point, but he didn't lack for communication skills. And then he looked in the direction of my partner, who of course was the host of this shoot. The guide waited for instructions. Interestingly, my partner only shrugged in the direction of the guide. You're on your own here, pal, he seemed to be saying. The guide returned his gaze to me. There was a con-fidence in his eyes. After all, we were in his element here, not mine. Our eyes locked again.

We were two cavemen, loinclothed, facing each other over a burning campfire. Prehistoric animals lurked just out of sight. Language had not yet been invented. The struggle between us was monumental, life and death. We glared at each other, bared our teeth. . . . Okay, okay, the guide was just really pissed off at me because I was interfering with his job. And I was pissed off at him because of his smelly dog. But for a moment there, it felt as though I had been catapulted back in time, to the dawn of man, when all our ancestors' every move was laced with the constant struggle between life and death.

"Can't," the guide said to me once again. His eyes told me all I needed to know. He'd won this contest. He'd beaten me. Here he was, a hired hunting guide, and he'd beaten me, a fancy-pants lawyer. That's when I pulled my trump card.

"Throw the dog out of the blind," I repeated to the guide as I removed the safety from my shotgun.

The guide's eyes widened. I got a few more blinks from him. What in hell? he was thinking. You wouldn't shoot my dog over a few farts, now would you?

And, of course, I had no intention of shooting his dog. Him? Well . . . No, I wasn't about to do anything of the sort. But the guide was uncertain. This was, after all, only a hunting party.

So, with a shrug I can only describe as theatric, the guide finally reached over, grabbed the dog by the scruff of its neck, rose out of the blind, and threw it onto the field. Just as he did so, we all saw a formation of geese overhead, headed straight our way. Headed straight our way, that is, until they saw the dog come flying out of our blind. (Geese have great eyesight.) Then they quickly changed direction and headed in formation away from our blind and toward another open field.

We heard the pop, pop, pop of the hunters' shotguns in that adjacent field as they downed the geese we had sent their way.

The guide looked at me. Satisfied, now? he was clearly thinking. But all I could think of was my still chronic need for air. I rose from the blind and took three or four deep breaths of fresh, plentiful farm air. God, isn't this just wonderful, don't you just love this? my face said, as I turned back toward my hunting comrades-in-arms. They were staring at me. No, they weren't staring at me. They were glaring at me. Silently, each and every one of them. Just then, the dog slowly picked himself up, walked a few feet out into the field, and took a big dump. Then, and without even turning around to see what we were all up to, he slowly walked away toward the trees at the far end of the farm. He seemed to know that his services would no longer be needed that day.

And he was right. While we all piled back into the blind—me apologizing all the way in—we never saw any more geese. I thought the guide showed a little too much pleasure when he announced to us after a couple of hours, "That's it, goin' home."

My partner was pretty gracious about it all. He never brought it up to me afterward, even invited me hunting again. Although his tone of voice made it clear that if I happened to have other plans that day, that'd be okay, too. I told him I'd love to go. But I had other plans that day.

I do get use out of my hunting clothes.

In snowstorms, I'm the guy dressed like the Delta Force commando.

R.L.

Nighttime Is the Right Time

I AM A PARTNER IN A LONDON FIRM OF SOLICITORS. TO MOST IN our profession, the word *partner* carries a wealth of meanings, but they all really translate to the same thing: I have made it. But I will not easily forget the early years.

A London junior solicitor's life is a mixture of pleasure and pain. The work is fascinating, and that is a great pleasure. Partnership looms ahead: the land of milk and honey. But the pain is never far from sight, with all-night meetings, cold, greasy conference-room pizza, the last-minute deal requiring breakneck labors. It usually begins with a call. Let's go back in time.

It is Friday afternoon. The day had started well enough. That morning, on the way to work, I had taken advantage of a sale at an Oriental-carpet store to purchase a small Turkish rug . . . a runner. I took it to the office, intending to bring it home that evening. I phoned my wife and told her I might leave a bit early, get a start on the weekend. Minutes later, my phone rings.

A partner calls.

"Could you possibly be available to assist on a project?"

I know that tone of voice. It means "immediately; I shall expect you to drop everything."

I try not to let him hear me sigh.

"Of course," I say.

I call my wife, now audibly sighing as I dial. Before she picks up, I silently rehearse my apology.

The client was a property group, always short of cash, run by a man who had played soccer at very nearly World Cup level. He had been a defensive player, notoriously mean and aggressive, characteristics he retained in commercial life. The deal was a complicated sale of property owned by the client and mortgaged to a bank. It was a deal with substantial tax advantages, but only if it could be done that day, before midnight, the end of the bank's financial year.

The partner told me to stand by. He made it clear that he had no intention of giving up his Friday evening.

"I expect it'll all fall through anyway," he said. He mentioned the agent who had set up the deal. "Everything he does turns to shit as a matter of routine."

I wanted to believe it. But it didn't really matter. I returned to my office and waited, sadly eyeing my new rug, rolled, lying forlornly on the floor.

I was told which law firm the bank had instructed—a surprising choice, I thought. They mainly did shipping work. They were reported to be drafting away and would be ready for us with documentation at four o'clock. I was told we had to agree on the documentation by six o'clock because the executive director of the bank had a very important prior engagement.

I called my wife. "I've got a runner, for the hall floor," I said; my way of telling her not to expect me anytime soon. She knew my tone of voice; I'm certain she got the meaning of what I *didn't* say.

Four o'clock. We were all in the bank's conference room. I had brought another young solicitor, named George, from our office. Our client, the man who nearly defended for England, was there. So was the agent, whose deal had apparently *not* turned to shit. We met the solicitors representing the bank, two rather young lawyers called Hugo and James. And of course, their client, the man with the prior engagement, a visibly distraught banker named Gerald.

Hugo proudly produced his draft documents and we read them. They had evidently been done in a great hurry. Equally clearly, they had been adapted from shipping agreements; the front end was fine, but the rest was filled with maritime references. George sighed. He too now clearly saw the night ahead.

I drew Hugo's attention to this privately, so as not to embarrass him. I needn't have worried; he was unembarrassable. I tried a more direct approach.

"We'll never do this by six," I said.

"Of course not," he said, with more enthusiasm than I thought helpful.

Gerald the banker sulked. (I later learned that he had sent his wife away for the weekend and was intent on spending some quality time with a new friend, Jane something-or-other.) His lawyer's aggressive willingness to spend the entire night in this conference room visibly affected Gerald. It was a pity his own lawyers didn't notice this. Gerald's temper was not improved by the departure of my client, who announced that he would return after an important evening engagement, after which he expected to find something ready to sign.

Seven o'clock. By now Gerald the banker was in a serious sulk. Our client had escaped. Gerald decided no one else would get away. If *he* was going to stay, and miss the warm open arms of Jane something-or-other, so were we. End of story.

To each and every point that came up Gerald simply said no. The agent did not help matters. Most such agents would have left us to it, but this one was determined to stay and protect his 10 percent commission. Possibly he had dealt with our client before. Not content, however, with sticking around, he was full of foolish suggestions for the wording of the documents.

Nine o'clock. Gerald was in a bad way. He had done some mental calculations, plotting the number of pages of the draft documents left to go. At the rate we were going this would take until dawn. Jane would be waking up alone in the morning.

"Totally unacceptable," he kept saying, meaning my latest proposal, his predicament, the world. Hugo had a good idea. He brought him some whiskey. Gerald still looked desperate, but he said no less often.

Ten o'clock. We called for pizzas . . . a selection. Clients get first choice. I ended up with the ham and pineapple. On the dot of eleven the agent made an announcement.

"I never leave a deal unclosed," he said, "but I never stay up after eleven o'clock either. I will lie down, but I will not sleep." He lay on the floor and thereafter pontificated from a supine position.

Ten to twelve. I remembered that the deal had to be done by midnight or the tax benefits wouldn't work. Panicked, I told the others.

"It's okay, so long as we finish the deal, and the papers, in this session. We can go on all night," said Hugo, still not embarrassed.

Midnight. My client returned. He was flushed with the effects of his important evening engagement. But although he made a token complaint that we hadn't finished, he entered the fray with enthusiasm, striding around the room and sidestepping the agent on the floor, using the footwork with which he had almost represented his country on the soccer field.

Two o'clock. My colleague George was coming into his own. Every time we would dispose of some point at issue, he would furrow his brow and say, "I don't think that's quite right, though, is it?"

For just a moment, I may have seriously considered murder.

Hugo suddenly went quiet. It had been a long day for him. He might have fallen asleep. Fortunately, he had James to take over. I suppose it was the same with George and me; you need someone to take the strain in an all-night meeting.

Three o'clock. We found ourselves arguing heatedly over some words that, as Gerald of all people pointed out, were totally meaningless. "It's not even as if there was something that they might mean," he said. There was some giggling. Hugo, now awake again, went and made some coffee.

At four, to our surprise, it was suddenly all done. This was in the days before we could all manipulate the word-processing system; it had to be typed. The lawyer for the client parting with the money has that responsibility. That meant that all of us, except Hugo, could get a few hours' sleep. We would reconvene after Hugo had the agreements typed.

At this point in the transaction there is a great feeling of camaraderie, of an important experience shared. We stood around joking, deferring the moment of departure. Someone rang for cabs, but it turned out that I lived in the same general direction as my client and he offered me a lift in his BMW. He was at peace with the world; he had just landed two million pounds sterling.

"That's nice," he said as I put the runner I had bought in his back seat.

"It's a runner," I said. "It's Turkish."

"Right," he said, clearly less impressed than I had hoped.

Dawn was breaking over West London. It was a lovely sight. As we sped through the deserted streets he confided in me details of his early struggles, his background, his aspirations, now never to be realized, to represent his country.

"The Premier League [a kind of English major league] was never enough for me," he said.

I can only ask that you imagine my state of mind upon arriving home: severe lassitude, caused by extreme exhaustion, mellowed by a no doubt transient feeling of professional accomplishment and the quiet of a predawn London street. Imagine, then, the shock to my system when greeted by a scene of complete pandemonium. Police cars had surrounded the place and a man was hammering at the door. My client, a man of action, leaped from the car and tackled the man just as the police did. My wife stood there in tears.

She said, "He kept banging on the door and shouting, 'I've got the runner! I've got the runner!' I thought he'd killed you for it."

I indicated the rug, which was safely under my arm, together with the final version of the documents.

"I'll kill him," said my client, which I must confess, I really appreciated. At the time, the man remained a mystery, though he was clearly drunk. At any rate, the police hauled him away. My client left and I then went in for breakfast and an hour's sleep.

Later that morning, we all reconvened in the bank's conference room. Gerald the banker had obviously made good use of his time away. He gave every appearance of being in love. As we checked the documents for any remaining typos, the police called. It turned out that the man pounding at my door, shouting about the runner, had referred not to a rug, suitable for a corridor, but to a horse, which he had backed, and which had won. Inebriated though he may have been, he was simply trying to share his good luck with the neighborhood. (I glimpsed lessons for a lawyer, having to do with unambiguous use of language, but I was too tired to care.)

The papers finished, we all shook hands. By now we were no longer comrades-in-arms.

It was, after all, Saturday morning. We needed to get some rest.

Monday was close at hand.

And, of course, the next partner's call.

Robin Bynoe
Charles Russell, Solicitors
London, England

Goodbye Law, Hello Life

I SENSED THAT LAWYERING WASN'T FOR ME DURING MY FIRST year of law school.

In Criminal Procedure, my professor interrupted his lecture to deliver a sermon. I don't know to this day what prompted him to divert from the course materials, but the point of the sermon was clear enough. We could be one of two things in life, he said: lawyers or poets. But not both. When I heard this, seated in the back row of the lecture hall, I was busy writing an outline for a short story (or was it a business plan?) in the margin of my casebook. I looked up. I felt exposed. But then the professor went back to the course materials. I began paying attention.

Three years later I graduated and passed the bar.

For about four years after that, I practiced law, all the while secretly plotting my escape. I was an associate in a major law firm. I worked like a dog. That I didn't mind. It was just that the work didn't satisfy my inner desires. Then, just as a major case I was working on came to an end, I quit. My wife and I decided to realize our dreams by moving to Israel. To my surprise, no one tried to talk me out of it. As I explained my reasons to the partners for whom I worked, each slipped into a reminiscence of his own dreams at my age. They did not want to stand in my way.

Israel seemed the perfect setting in which to abandon my occupational albatross. We started in a kibbutz. Early the first day I presented myself to the work assignment secretary. Everything seemed right. There was no sign of starched shirts, no dark suits, no attaché cases. And here I was, educated (with two degrees, mind you) and ready to do my share. I was welcomed to the kibbutz, handed a broom, and instructed to sweep the floor of the plastics factory. Then, when I finished, I could continue outside. A somewhat disappointing start, I must admit, but I was determined to do my best. And I did. I also threw my back out.

After a few days of recovery, aided by painkillers and a sympathetic wife, I was next assigned to the organic fields. Organic farming. Here, I thought, was the perfect existential antidote for all of the trees that had been felled for my legal briefs and yellow legal pads. Here was the reward for my patience and perseverance. On my first assignment, accompanied by a fellow new immigrant from Slovakia, I was transported in the early morning darkness to a distant site. We worked for a few hours in the dark. Once the sun came up and the flies arrived en masse, I realized that the essence of working in the organic fields was, well . . . shoveling shit. But I did it.

After the kibbutz, I entered an intensive Hebrew language course. I was the lone English speaker. The rest of the class was from the former Soviet Union. One day a work counselor arrived and told us the great opportunities we had to find a new life, to switch gears at mid-career. Finally, someone talking my language. Well, sort of my language. She was speaking in Hebrew and I could just make out what she seemed to be saying. Nonetheless, armed with this inspiration, I lined up some interviews with companies and organizations. I should confess that it was initially sufficiently thrilling for me to succeed in using my primitive Hebrew just to set up the meetings and answer questions at an interview. But it seemed that most of the interviews ended the same way.

"You seem very nice, but we don't have any positions for lawyers."

Perhaps something was lost in translation. I thought I had made it clear that I was applying for the advertised position: in marketing, in administration, in whatever they were looking for. While waiting for call-back interviews that never came, I resigned myself to my apparent fate as a lawyer for life and began the lengthy retraining, testing, and apprenticeship for foreign lawyers sponsored by the Israel Bar Association.

My albatross had refastened itself around my neck.

I started my renewed legal career in historic Nazareth. According to the New Testament, Nazareth was where Jesus spent his childhood and Mary received the Annunciation. As I passed through the narrow streets of the old city, I was captivated by the inviting scents from storefronts, passing donkey carts, and cardamom-scented coffee. Somehow, I sensed my arrival was hardly noteworthy.

The district prosecutor's office for the northern Galilee region seemed to recognize my professional plight but not my legal potential. Nonetheless, the head prosecutor conceded that some of my U.S. legal experience might be helpful, and since a Russian immigrant lawyer was also just starting, maybe she and I could help each other. The two of us quickly sensed our common failing in a part of the world where no one seemed to need a license (or courtroom) to commence a street-side public inquiry or tribunal. In comparison to the proper court settings of our respective former countries, the judicial environment here appeared more like a local market, characterized by informal bargaining and colorful arguments, than a courtroom. I realized that the local cucumber trader was probably a more effective advocate than either of us would ever be.

Before long I was once again writing outlines for business plans and short stories in the margins of my legal pad.

This time my escape from the legal world was instigated by a different kind of force. The rural location of the prosecutor's office was often used as an excuse for the poor state of its computer system in 1995. We had the functional equivalent of a typing pool, but each time I handed in a second draft of a document, I noticed that the secretary simply retyped the entire document on the computer, instead of making corrections. One day as I approached our computer consultant with a routine question, I noticed that her computer screen was uncharacteristically filled with English text and graphics. More surprisingly, the text was information from the U.S. Library of Congress. When I learned that this was an online Internet site, that her computer was connected to a place I assumed I had abandoned forever, I was forced to reassess my basic assumptions about my physical isolation. As was happening to so many others, a whole new world had opened up to me.

I was able to explore this new technology further when I finally received a call-back interview for an ill-defined position at the Technion—the Israel Institute of Technology. I quickly accepted, and during the next several years earned an unofficial degree in the new information order. Suddenly, my skills seemed to have a new image and value to me and to others as well.

In this globalized high-tech world, I started immediately to run into other ex-lawyers. While some refer to themselves as "recovering" lawyers, I noticed that former lawyers get a rush out of discussing what they call the absurdity of the old days. It's really strange. Here we were, escapees. Happy to be out, yet full of nostalgia for the old days.

As I reflect on this today, I think my law professor was wrong in forcing us to choose a single identity—lawyer or poet. Technology (and old-fashioned human nature) will continue to diminish the distinctions of our established professions.

These days, I work with start-up Israeli high-tech companies as a consultant, entrepreneur, and yes, sometimes even as a lawyer. As I sit here in this Mediterranean mosaic of ancient and modern, familiar and yet to be discovered, the categorizations just don't seem so important anymore.

WAYNE L. FIRESTONE
CHIEF EXECUTIVE OFFICER
SILICON WADINET, LTD.
WEST GALILEE, ISRAEL

He Gave Him the Finger

Many a criminal case is solved by use of a fingerprint identification.

As a Deputy DA in Colorado Springs, I had the mother of all fingerprint cases.

The defendant broke into a liquor store, smashing the plate-glass window. He climbed into the store and took what he wanted before fleeing the scene. Thing was he somehow had managed to cut a part off his finger on the broken glass.

An hour or so later, he showed up at the local hospital emergency room—minus a part of his you-know-what.

Wisely, he decided to plead guilty.

I mean, after all, we not only had the fingerprints.

We had the finger.

Thomas A. Barnes, Jr.
Attorney at Law
Colorado Springs, Colorado

Give Me a Break

[Editor's note: I received at least two versions of what follows. The letters in question are among those that circulate from lawyer to lawyer. The identity of the actual author(s) was apparently unknown to those who passed the story on to me. I chose and edited the one I liked the best. The lawyer who sent it to me said that in fairness she shouldn't have her name on it since she didn't write it.]

A NEW ORLEANS LAWYER SOUGHT AN FHA LOAN FOR A client. He was told the loan would be granted if he could prove satisfactory title to a parcel of property being offered as collateral. The title to the property dated back to 1803, which took the lawyer three months to track down. After sending the information to the FHA, he received the following reply (actual letter):

> Reviewing your letter adjoining your client's loan application, we note that the request is supported by an Abstract of Title. While we compliment the able manner in which you have prepared and presented the application, we must point out that you have only cleared title to the proposed collateral property back to 1803. Before final approval can be accorded, it will be necessary to clear the title back to its origin.

Annoyed, the lawyer responded as follows (actual letter):

> Your letter regarding title in Case No. 189156 has been received. I note that you wish to have title extended further than the 194 years covered by the present application. I was unaware that any educated person in this country, particularly those working in the property area, would not

know that Louisiana was purchased by the U.S. from France in 1803, the year of origin identified in our application. For the edification of uninformed FHA bureaucrats, the title to the land prior to U.S. ownership was obtained from France, which had acquired it by Right of Conquest from Spain. The land came into possession of Spain by Right of Discovery made in the year 1492 by a sea captain named Christopher Columbus, who had been granted the privilege of seeking a new route to India by the then reigning monarch, Isabella. The good queen, being a pious woman and careful about titles, almost as much as the FHA, took the precaution of securing the blessing of the Pope before she sold her jewels to fund Columbus' expedition.

Now the Pope, as I'm sure you know, is the emissary of Jesus Christ, the Son of God. And God, it is commonly accepted, created this world. Therefore, I believe it is safe to presume that He also made that part of the world called Louisiana. He, therefore, would be the owner of origin. I hope to hell you find His original claim to be satisfactory.

Now, may we have our damn loan?

They got it.

First Footing

ONE DARK AND DREARY AFTERNOON IN LATE NOVEMBER I was about to leave my London law office when I received a call from a client in Houston. Could I handle the legal formalities for a multimillion-dollar repayment of capital by the client's British subsidiary?

"Sure," I replied, confident that even I could manage a straightforward internal, corporate-to-corporate transaction.

Then the problem appeared. For tax reasons, the parent corporation in Texas needed the deal to close no later than December 31. However, the timetable laid down by British legislation would not permit the U.K. subsidiary to close the transaction earlier than January 1.

Eventually, the answer dawned on me. We had to use that window when it's still December 31 in Texas, but it's January 1 in Britain; a closing by phone and fax sometime between midnight and 6 A.M. New Year's Eve.

That year, I spent the New Year's holiday at my mother-in-law's home on the Scottish island of Skye. I came properly prepared with a portable fax machine and a shiny new ledger book in which to record the movement of millions of dollars safely held in my firm's trust account from the U.K. subsidiary to that of the U.S. corporate parent.

Now, New Year's Eve (or Hogmanay, as the Scots call it) is the major holiday in Scotland—bigger even than Christmas. But the Scots don't celebrate Hogmanay by going out to parties or dinners. Traditionally, they stay at home quietly imbibing the national drink until the clock strikes midnight. Then it's a frantic rush to "first foot" as many neighbors as possible.

"First footing" is achieved by being the first person in the new year to cross a neighbor's threshold bearing food, drink, and coal. The symbolism is obvious, and the occasion is typically accompanied by great merriment, the playing of bagpipes, and, of course, meaningful consumption of the national drink.

My mother-in-law is quite a popular lady, so we had no shortage of first footers. I am not sure who were most surprised—the businessmen in Houston, huddled around a speakerphone, who were subjected to a closing that appeared to be taking place in a drunken orgy; or the Scottish first-footers who witnessed an Englishman, drink in hand, wrestling with a complex legal opinion dealing with such arcane issues as the legal status of Greenwich Mean Time.

Fortunately, when I looked at the documents in the cold light of morning, they seemed to make sense.

And eventually, my headache went away.

IAN FAGELSON
WARNER CRANSTON
LONDON, ENGLAND

You're a Lawyer, Right?

YOU'RE A LAWYER, RIGHT?"

That's the one question guaranteed to make a lawyer cringe.

It's an off-duty question. You're not at your law office. You hear it at parties. Or it's hurled across dinner tables by some other guest—one who's been staring at you for the last hour with undisguised contempt. Sometimes it comes from the driver of a taxicab, while you're being held captive in the back seat.

On occasion it's nothing more than a play for free legal advice. All things considered, that's not too bad. I mean, after all, why not try to see if you can save yourself a trip to your lawyer's office and the consequent bill in the mail? But the question usually means that the lawyer is about to be confronted with someone who is angry or frustrated with something personal—on occasion irrational—and the lawyer is about to get an earful.

Here you are, out for an evening with your spouse or your friends. What you want is a little R&R away from your law office. And what do you get? You get subjected to some jerk who's now going to complain at length about something or other about which you couldn't give a . . .

So when we lawyers hear the question—well, we tighten up.

Last time I tightened up, I was in a cab, headed home from work.

It was a spring evening, not yet too hot, still light out. I was aimlessly looking out the window, enjoying the short ride home.

"You're a lawyer, right?"

My gaze shot to the rearview mirror. A pair of eyes were watching, darting between the traffic and me. I sighed. Here we go, I almost said out loud.

We lawyers aren't hard to spot. We have a certain sameness to us, with our dark suits and, with some exceptions, conservative hairstyles. And if you happened to be in a rush-hour cab in Washington, D.C., where I live, chances are way better than fifty-fifty that you're a lawyer.

The eyes in the rearview mirror were waiting for a response.

The cabbie looked to be in his sixties. African-American. Gray hair thinned to the point of balding. I could see that he was thin. He wore a patterned short-sleeved shirt, exposing wiry, veined arms and bony hands. (In D.C., the majority of cabdrivers are recent immigrants and speak little or no English. And usually can't find anything.) This guy spoke accentless English. And he seemed angry. Oh boy, I thought.

The eyes in the rearview mirror said, So, are you?

"Yes," I said with the unmistakable tone of someone cornered.

The cabbie was silent as he negotiated the rush-hour traffic. Could it be that his only interest was in pegging the occupations of his fares? Nothing more? I began to relax. Then came the second question.

"Why they let him go?"

Of course I had no idea what he meant. I began silently debating how best to navigate the short ride home, without having to be subjected to a barrage of questions seeking legal advice, or to some crazy diatribe about how someone had cheated this guy. I checked the street signs at the intersection we were passing, trying to clock the distance to my house.

I didn't ask who had let him (whoever he was) go. I just grunted something unintelligible, a kind of short version of "Uh-huh. I understand. Sure. Whatever you say."

I watched the rearview mirror. The driver seemed to be studying me, as though he was trying to decide something. Here we go, I thought. What's it going to be this time? A used-car sale gone bad? Maybe a fender bender between his cab and another driver?

But the cabbie was still silent, still seemingly studying me through his end of the mirror.

And then he spoke. And I listened.

The driver's only child, a daughter, was bright. A good girl. Just like her mother. She had graduated from her inner-city high school as valedictorian, with a full scholarship to Morehouse College. It happened during the summer between her freshman and sophomore years. And there was nothing anyone could do to stop it.

She had a boyfriend. He too was from the neighborhood, had gone to the same high school. And while he may not have been the scholar that the cabbie's daughter was, he also had received a college scholarship. His was for athletics, football, the driver said.

They had dated in high school, had kept in touch while away at college, and had spent the early part of their first summer at home, pretty much inseparable.

He seemed like a nice boy, the driver said. He was over at the house a lot, was always polite and respectable, never a problem. He wore nice clothes. Expensive, actually. And he drove a BMW. The cabbie should have paid more attention to that, he told me. The boy didn't have a summer job, and yet he had all this money. He took the girl out for nice dinners and to fancy dance clubs. But he was so polite, and so nice to his daughter, the fact that he was a drug dealer never occurred to him, the cabbie said. But I could hear it in his voice, see it in his eyes, as they beseeched me through the rearview mirror. He knew it should have occurred to him. Probably did, in some subconscious, denial kind of way.

We drove for another block or so in silence, although I don't think the cabbie realized this, he was so absorbed in memories of his daughter. I said nothing, waiting for him to continue.

"You got kids, mister?" the driver asked, finally breaking the silence.

I told him I did, but I didn't elaborate. I could see that this question was simply his way of reverbalizing. He was coming to the most painful part of the story.

A summer night, just like any other. The boy had come over to the house just as he, his wife, and daughter were finishing supper. Would you like something to eat? his wife had asked. No, ma'am, he had said, explaining that he had just finished supper at his own house. And besides, they were going to a movie that evening and they didn't want to be late. So their daughter left the dinner table to go upstairs and quickly get ready. The boy sat there, smiling, talking about sports, how he was enjoying his summer, as the cabbie's wife cleared the table.

A few moments later, his daughter bounded down the stairs and, after a quick good night to her parents, she and the boy were outside on their way to the movies. His wife was washing the dishes in the kitchen, he had just sat down with the newspaper, when they heard the unmistakable sounds. He knew immediately, all the while hoping—no, praying—that he was wrong, that it was something else he had heard.

Three, no, *four* pops, all in quick succession, then the squeal of tires.

His wife left the kitchen. She stood there in the living room, wet dish towel still in her hands, looking at him. Saying with her eyes, no, no, not our baby. Please, Lord, no. He rose from the chair. His wife behind him, he opened the door. Of course, his worst fears were there, out on the street in front of his house, just as he knew they would be.

Just as his daughter and the boy were at his car, about to get in, another car, one that had been waiting, made its approach. A rival drug gang. Prior insults. Turf disputes. The cabbie didn't know which. After, the police had been full of explanations. But by then he was only half listening, being strangely polite to the police. Calling them sir and thanking them. When inside he had such rage, he himself could have killed.

The boys in the passing car had fired. The boyfriend had apparently seen them just as they were taking aim. He dove for the ground, his car shielding him. The cabbie's daughter had no idea what was about to happen. She became the target. Three shots had hit her, the cabbie told me. One to the head, one in the stomach, one in the arm. All high-velocity bullets. They tore her apart, he said. By the time he got to her, she was already dead. His baby was dead. Mutilated by those gunshots.

As his wife stood above him, shrieking, he cradled his daughter's body, gently rocking her, telling her, baby, it'll be okay, you gonna be all right. We here. We here with you, baby. As all this was happening, he saw the boy. It was safe for him to get up from where he was still lying.

"Strange what you notice, mister," the cabbie told me. "What you see when you holdin' your dead child in your arms, her blood runnin' all over you. Her beautiful face torn up. You hear your wife standin' beside you, cryin', screamin' for her child. All this happenin', and here's this boy. I see him slowly get up from where he's lyin'. He's checkin' out the street, wantin' to make sure them other boys're gone. That he's safe. I watch him slowly dust himself off. When he gets to it, he sees my baby lyin' there. But he don't do nothin'. He looks away. I see him lookin' down the street again. He's decidin'. Do I stay, or do I run? How do I handle this when the cops come? It's like he don't even notice me, or my baby. No, he's only thinkin' 'bout how he's gonna handle this."

The cops did eventually come, the cabbie said. The boy stayed. Everyone gave statements to the police. The police knew the boy. Knew he sold drugs. But he was unarmed. They searched him. No drugs. So after a while, after the ambulance came and went, after the neighbors returned to their houses, after all that, the police let the boy go home. He never said a word to the parents. Never even looked at them. When the police told him he could leave, he quietly crossed the street, left his car for the police to extract the fourth bullet, and walked home.

By now the cab was approaching my house. The driver slowed until I told him to stop, that we were there. But I didn't leave the cab. Both of us were silent, seated one behind the other. Strange, I later realized. The cabbie never once turned around in his seat to look at me. Our only eye contact was through that mirror. There was a kind of barrier to it. We were there, together in the confined space of the man's cab. We talked. Mostly, I listened. We exchanged glances. Yet it was as though, somehow, he and I were in two separate spaces. And for some reason, I later realized, the driver wanted it that way. I'm still not sure why.

They never caught the shooters, the cabbie said. And the boy . . . well, nothing ever happened to him either. At summer's end, he went back to college. After a while, I awkwardly fumbled in my pocket for some cash to pay the driver. He kept watching me, not yet interested in accepting his fare. There was one more question he wanted to ask.

"Why the law do that, mister?" he said. "Why it let them take my baby, and then go on about their business, like nothin' at all happened?"

I said I didn't know. Said it was all terrible, how sorry I was. That it was wrong. All wrong.

As I handed the driver his fare, and as he thanked me, he continued to watch me through the mirror. I left the cab. There was nothing more to be said. He recorded the fare on his daily log. Then he drove away.

I stood on the sidewalk for a while, thinking about what had just happened. This was not the first time the man had told that story to someone in his cab. His story had, I realized, the air of an exercise, something he routinely did. And then I realized why.

It was all he *could* do. He was powerless before the law. Like most people. At its mercy. His daughter had been taken from him and those responsible were walking the streets. All the man could do was tell the story. Over and over. Especially to lawyers. Those of us duty-bound to uphold the law. He would let us know, day in and day out, how the law had let him down. He would educate us. Maybe the next time one of us would be in a position to help the next person. To the cabbie we lawyers were the only people not powerless before the law.

I've thought about that cabbie. Out there somewhere, driving his shift, watching the men and women of my profession as they seat themselves in the rear seat of his cab. Waiting until they've settled in. Then asking:

"You're a lawyer, right?"

And I must confess, when someone else confronts me with that question now, I listen, wondering if I'm about to meet another person abandoned by the law.

R.L.

And in Clause III(D), The Booties

I WAS ON MATERNITY LEAVE FROM A POWERHOUSE NEW YORK firm, and it was an eerie transition. Life went quiet. No longer did I manage the interrupting office phone, close study of the tax law, or international trust agreements that had to be signed by midnight. Now I handled sporadic howls, the study of nursery texts, and changing the diaper before I got squirted in the eye.

I could do law for a stretch. I could do baby care for a stretch. I hadn't yet done both in one day. But the moment had come. I had a date with the judge. The Surrogate's Court had scheduled a hearing, and I was to be present. And I had not been a lawyer mother before.

I found a sitter and checked every possible reference. I packed my son's bag. Early in the morning of the big event—and I don't mean the motion scheduled for 10:00 A.M.—I drove to the sitter's house to drop him off. I don't say "drop off" literally, because it took a lot longer than that.

"Don't forget to feed him," I told the sitter sternly.

"Yes, ma'am," she said.

"Don't forget to let him sleep," I instructed.

"Yes, ma'am," she said.

"Is this where he takes a nap?" I asked suspiciously.

"Yes, ma'am," she said. "We call that a crib."

"What about this plastic toy?" I asked critically, pointing to her toy box. "Is this safe?"

"Yes, ma'am," she said. "It's exactly like the one you have in your bag."

Dubious, I abandoned my poor child. Mysteriously, he didn't cry at all. Three minutes later I had parked the car at the Greenwich station, ready for the 7:18. Calmly, I opened my briefcase to review the court papers.

Which was when it struck me. Deep, I might add, in the heart. I hadn't told her to *warm my son's bottle* before she gave it to him!

I dug into my wallet for change. I ran, flustered, to the pay phone and called. "Don't forget to warm the bottle," I said specifically, as the train chugged into the station.

"Yes, ma'am," she said.

On the express, I reread our motion argument. But something was seriously wrong. I hadn't—yes, I admit it, I imagined myself shamefacedly explaining to the senior partner—I hadn't told her to burp him! And he needed it!

Arriving at Grand Central, I found a pay phone and dialed.

"Do not," I stated in language worthy of a major legal contract, "forget to burp him!"

"Yes, ma'am," she said.

What a relief. I took the subway downtown. You can probably guess what happened. When I got to the Surrogate's Court, I practically knocked over the security guard seeking directions to the pay phone. He told me where to find it. "Gotta call your boss, eh?" he said.

In a way he was right. I dialed the sitter in panic.

"Don't forget," I told her, "to change his diaper!"

"Yes, ma'am," she said. "He's doing fine. But you seem kind of nervous. Is this your first time with a sitter?"

"How did you know?" I asked, dumbfounded.

In the courtroom, I reviewed the facts. I was an experienced lawyer. I routinely tackled challenging emergencies. Surely, I told myself, I could forget my eight-week-old son for twenty minutes.

I did, because at our hearing, unexpected opposition showed up with a challenge—to our legal fee.

Son? Diapers, you say? Are you talking about somebody else? I defended our position ably. After the hearing, I got on the phone and explained the complexities to the senior partner. We calculated what to do next. I walked out of the courtroom and took the subway back uptown, thinking about the case. It wasn't until I was two blocks from my office that I remembered the partner wasn't even expecting me and I was supposed to go home.

Home? Wasn't there somebody waiting for me?

But I didn't call the sitter on the ride back. No, I put my feet up and relaxed. She had probably taken the phone off the hook anyway. When I got to her house, my son flapped his little hand at me casually. Like nothing had happened.

I guess nothing had.

MARTHA B. G. LUFKIN, ESQUIRE
LINCOLN, MASSACHUSETTS

Puerto Rican Interlude

San Juan, Puerto Rico. A sultry day. A sense of holiday and adventure spreads through the cabin as my plane approaches the island with its green waters and white beaches. Latin America meets the United States. But I'm not on vacation. For me, this trip is strictly business.

It's March 1966. I have left private practice in Washington, D.C., to become international in-house counsel to Sears Roebuck & Company. Sears de Puerto Rico has become one of the fastest-growing of the company's Latin American operations.

Sears has problems in Peru, Brazil, and Panama, but nothing like what is happening in Puerto Rico. The new store in Caguas is under way, without, it seems, a construction permit (not an uncommon occurrence on the island). In the meantime, a local Department of Commerce study has claimed that Sears' proposed new store will result in the bankruptcy of dozens of small local businesses. There is a definite sense of tension in the air. A major mainland corporation is invading the island, jeopardizing the livelihoods of the local merchants. A do-or-die court hearing has been scheduled.

Back in Chicago, at Sears corporate headquarters, the international operations department has become a staging ground in preparation for the hearing. Numerous disciplines are brought into play, all designed to put the most compelling case together to justify opening the Puerto Rican store.

It is with this background that I leave on Tuesday, March 22, 1966, for San Juan, for preparatory action on the Caguas issue. I have a substantial agenda. Meetings are to be held with the president of Sears de Puerto Rico, construction experts, economic advisers, and outside lawyers.

Commuting between Chicago and San Juan, I return the following Wednesday, March 30, for a meeting with the Puerto Rican secretary of commerce and his staff. The meeting is friendly but there are political problems with the opposition of the small businesses. The matter is further complicated by disputes over the size of the store and the extent of its impact. Sears commits to assist in training, and is flexible on size.

The stage is set for court action on Thursday. The secretary of commerce has apparently advised the Planning Board that he is now leaning favorably toward Sears' entry into Caguas. A new report is promised.

In court, after a period of preliminary skirmishing between counsel, the judge calls a sudden recess for a meeting in his chambers with Sears' local counsel. It is unclear what the flurry of activity is about and why the need for an in-camera conference. Time passes, as the court stands in adjournment.

After what seems like a hospital-style waiting period, the Sears trial attorney reappears for a huddled conference with those of us from Chicago.

Counsel calmly explains that the judge had a serious complaint—he had overpaid his Sears credit account and had yet to receive a credit. Needless to say, after a series of phone calls within a very short period of time, the credit account is checked out and the refund is on its way. Sears was clearly in error.

The permits are issued later in the afternoon. Simple as that.

Back on the plane, I look out the window at the disappearing island. I think about how much I'd like a vacation.

PATRICK J. HEAD
ALTHEIMER & GRAY
CHICAGO, ILLINOIS

But She's Listed in the Telephone Directory

For a number of years I was involved in handling, under contract, all felony appeals in the county where I resided. Over time this amounted to nearly a thousand appeal cases.

On one occasion I successfully appealed the conviction of a man who had been tried and convicted of criminal sexual assault, first-degree (rape, in other words). The trial had featured a number of significant procedural errors, so the Court of Appeals was duly upset when, some years after the initial conviction, the case came to them on appeal. The appellate court reversed the conviction and sent the case back to the lower court for a new trial.

In time my client and I appeared before the lower court for the commencement of new proceedings, scheduling, and so on. At that point I reminded the now-reversed judge that my client was back at the beginning—meaning he was in a pretrial status. Hence, he had been reinvested with the cloak of innocence. That being the case, he was now entitled to the practical implication of that presumption—specifically, bond pending trial.

Obviously this predicament caused the judge some consternation, and he turned to the prosecutor for enlightenment. The prosecution rose to the occasion and venomous rhetoric spewed forth. She ridiculed the very notion of my client's being out on bond because his victim was still living in the community and was in mortal fear of my client, who undoubtedly would use his temporary release to attempt to harass her—maybe even repeat his previous crime. The prosecutor really got carried away, and she went on at some length about the danger posed to this poor victim if my client was out and about.

I listened to the prosecutorial harangue for some time and with some

amusement. When it was finally over, I stood and faced the court and confessed to my confusion. It was true—I observed—that indeed the victim
did "reside" in the community, but I was somehow uncertain as to how the
projected harm could occur, given the precise nature of her "residence."

"And what might that be?" inquired the court.

"Well, Your Honor," I replied, "the only residence that I am aware of
for the lady victim involved here is one that measures two feet by six feet
and lies buried under six feet of dirt. She 'resides' in a coffin—having been
totally dead for the last two and a half years."

Not one to give up, the prosecutor exclaimed, "But she's listed in the
telephone directory."

Bond was granted.

MILTON J. MAROVICH
ATTORNEY AT LAW
KALAMAZOO, MICHIGAN

Holy Krishna

POORLY JANITORED, WINDOWLESS, AND ILLUMINATED BY GRIMY fluorescence, the Phoenix City Magistrate's Court handled petty criminal offenses, most of which had occurred somewhere deep in inner-city squalor. In the late 1960s, arraignments were held every Tuesday morning for defendants charged during the preceding week with sex offenses or, as the florid bailiff put it, "with anything weird."

Walking down a hall littered with cigarette butts and filled with cops, dirty-shirt lawyers, and unhappy-looking people, my clients and I approached the door to courtroom number two and looked at the posted docket sheet. Evidently, it was going to be a typical Tuesday in Magistrate's Court: The schedule listed charges of prostitution ("hooking"), indecent exposure ("flag-waving"), and disturbing-the-peace-by-offensive-conduct, which is a euphemism for public urination ("DP-by-PeePee").

My clients were named at the bottom of the docket sheet and would be the last defendants to step up before Judge Benjamin Salt and enter a plea. The charge against them was "criminal trespass by loitering."

According to prosecutors, my four clients—all members of the International Society for Krishna Consciousness, or ISKCON—had "trespassed" at a large, privately owned shopping center. Heads shaved except for tufts in back, bodies clad in saffron robes, and foreheads painted with clay markings, the Hare Krishnas had encamped in a busy intersection between Sears and Penney, clanged small hand cymbals, beat on a drum, danced about, and endlessly chanted, "Hare Krishna, Hare Krishna, Krishna Krishna, Krishna Hare, Hare Hare, Hare Rama, Rama Rama, Hare Hare."

Vexed mall security officers demanded evacuation, the Hare Krishnas responded with more clanging and chanting, and the police arrived to make arrests. The Hare Krishnas' "loitering" was, according to the jargon in the criminal complaint, "inconsistent with the mall's express and implied invitation to engage in commerce."

Yet, as my vacant-eyed clients saw things, they had a "spiritual right" to be there and to spread "holy oneness." After all, they had not blocked foot traffic. They had only hawked an evangelistic tract, called *Back to Godhead,* that no mall merchant carried in inventory. They were pursuing their religious beliefs, not putting on a "freak show" as mall management had alleged. And last, their clangings and chantings were an artistic improvement over the mall's Muzak.

Upon entering the courtroom, my colorful entourage immediately drew stares from the sex offenders, derelicts, and everyone else present. As the five of us took our seats and all eyes stayed on us, I realized my mistake in loosely offering to do "any" free-speech case for the Arizona Civil Liberties Union.

Too old to be a 1960s radical, but too young to be a 1950s reactionary, I recently had graduated from Stanford Law School, joined a large Phoenix law firm, and entertained ambitions of handling high-profile "impact cases," preferably for professors, priests, rabbis, or ministers who opposed the Vietnam War. Not for a second did I imagine myself slumming in Magistrate's Court with a group of young men who looked like former potheads and who were so deviant that even trench-coated exhibitionists looked down on them and, at the same time, me.

Ignoring the looks glued on us, I pored over the legal treatises that I had brought with me and searched intensely for a Constitutional loophole. Somehow, I had to end this mortifying case, avoid any more courtroom snickers, and silence all the jokers back at the office.

Deep into the law books, I was jarred from my concentration by the judge's calling out my name, probably for the second or third time: "Mr. Baird, would you please approach the bench?" Rattled, I quickly walked up before Judge Salt, a bespectacled, round-faced man, who later, after years of adjudicating drunks and vice, would take his own life in despair.

"Come closer, Mr. Baird," Judge Salt directed, leaning toward me. "What are your clients doing?" he asked. "Well, Your Honor, they're waiting to plead not guilty to . . ." I started to say but was abruptly cut off by the judge, who said, "I know why they are here but *what* in the hell are they doing?"

It was then that I turned around and looked out onto the courtroom at what Judge Salt was seeing from his bench: four loony-looking young men who, with their eyes shut, were vigorously moving their right hands in the crotch region of their robes. "My God, Mr. Baird, they are playing with themselves in my courtroom," Judge Salt hissed, loud enough for almost everyone to hear except for my own clients, who apparently were in some other, more transcendental place.

"Holy Christ," I mumbled and, in four giant steps, was back to where my Hare Krishnas were seated, vigorously meditating. Shaking the nearest one by the shoulder and awakening them all from their trances, I tried in low tones to explain the situation, using euphemisms like "fooling around" and "privates." But either they couldn't hear or didn't understand because they kept asking me, with puzzled expressions, to repeat and explain. Meanwhile, the pressure mounted with every passing second, as all courtroom business stopped and the judge fidgeted impatiently.

After my whispered sputterings failed to convey the message, I finally surrendered to exasperation, abandoned all indirection, and to the criminal delight of the sex offenders and immense entertainment of everyone else within earshot, blurted out the *m* word.

According to what my clients told me later, they had been meditating and their hands had been innocently handling prayer beads in little lap bags. But, in the end, it didn't matter where their hands had been because I eventually found a loophole. The prosecutor was forced to drop all charges, although he evened the score with some parting comments about my clients' manipulations in Judge Salt's courtroom.

A few weeks after the case was dismissed, a receptionist called me and announced that there were "some very strange people here to see you." Without an appointment, my four Hare Krishnas had appeared in the firm's lobby. They were attracting stupefied looks from waiting clients and passing secretaries. As I approached, they greeted me with Gandhi-like gestures.

"We wanted to thank you for what you did for us," the eldest said, as he handed me a tinfoil package the size of a football and the weight of a small anvil. "It is our ceremonial bread," he explained, and then emphasized how all four of them had made the bread "with our own hands." Giving me only a moment to say something awkwardly polite, they quickly took their leave and the last I heard from them was the soft tinkle of a hand cymbal just as the elevator doors closed.

At home that night, I stared at the dense, grainy gift and wondered whether I was obliged to eat any of it—a piece of crust perhaps or maybe a few crumbs. I was relieved to have the case over and genuinely touched by their gesture. Still, I decided against even a nibble. After wrapping the ceremonial bread back up in the tinfoil, I lugged the package outside and dropped it into the trash can.

After all, I never was sure about that prayer bead story.

PETER D. BAIRD
LEWIS AND ROCA LLP
PHOENIX, ARIZONA

You German, Mate?

An American Lawyer's First Experience with European Soccer

As a trial lawyer, my practice has for years involved international work. A fair amount of it brings me regularly to London and puts me in the company of English lawyers. Some of them have become my friends. Once, while I was in London on my way back from the Middle East on business, a friend, a partner at one of London's top firms, called me and asked if I would like to join him and some of his colleagues in Barcelona for the European Cup soccer match. One of England's best teams, Manchester United, was scheduled to compete against a German team, Bayern Munich. England versus the Germans in a death-match struggle? This was better than court. Too good to miss. I said, Sure, wonderful, I'll be there. A small detour, I said, myself a World Cup rationalizer. This could be fun.

What it was, was a once-in-a-lifetime experience. I didn't attend a soccer match. Sure, it was that, too. More important, I had a ringside seat at a spectacle as intense and colorful as anything any ancient Roman got to watch at the Coliseum. True, no one died by sword or lion in Barcelona. I'd say that was about the only difference. It was as adversarial as adversarial can get.

First, a word about the teams. Each country has a national soccer team. Even we do. Most of you knew that, right? Okay, name three players on the U.S. team. Stumped, right? But real soccer—football to the rest of the world's population—resides in what I guess are called club teams. The club teams get the best players from all over the world—Brazilians, even Americans play for Dutch and German club teams. And the best of them return home to play for their national teams in World Cup play. Manchester United, from the Northern English city of Manchester, is one of these teams. They've been around a long time. Fans live and seemingly die on the fate of Man. U., as it's sometimes called, season after season. This year, Man. U. had won both of the two important English tournaments, the Premier Cup and the FA Cup (I had to ask, but FA stands for Football Association). If they could win the European Cup, then they would win the treble. This, believe me, is a real big deal.

The German Team, Bayern Munich, had also won its two important German cup matches. So they too were poised for the treble. And I can assure you, to judge by the noise in the stadium that evening, for them it was also a real big deal.

The German team is well known for its precision and its strength. Unlike the exuberant Manchester United team, who are filled with expressive—but at times undisciplined—players, the German team is all power. Maybe unimaginative, but soldierlike in their strength and dedication. All-powerful? Soldierlike? Oh boy, I say to myself as all this is being explained to me over a pregame late lunch in a lovely seafood restaurant overlooking Barcelona's beautiful harbor. Don't do it, I say to myself. Stay in the present. Don't drift back fifty years. Everybody's always doing this to the Germans. It's no longer fair. So to move the conversation along, I ask, what's *Bayern* mean? Bayern Munich, my luncheon companions explain, are from Bavaria. Bayern means Bavaria.

Bavaria? Munich? Isn't that where Hitler and the Nazi party got their first solid stronghold of support in prewar Germany? Sure it is, I almost whisper to myself. These players and their fans are the sons—or is it grandsons now?—of those early party followers. Stop, I command myself. Not fair. I remark on how good the food is here in Barcelona. And the view. Wow, get a look at that view, I tell my English lawyer companions. I think I notice a sideways glance or two, like, what's with him anyway? But the moment passes and soon we leave the restaurant for the subway and the stadium on the outskirts of town.

That's when I see the real fans. The diehards. Both the Brits and the Germans, working-class all, crowded in the same subway car with us.

First a word about us. Then a word about them. We—except for me, the Yank—are upper-class, educated Englishmen. No less Man. U. fans. Just different. We're quiet. We are feeling good from the wine at lunch, but there are no lukewarm cans of beer clasped in our fists. We are wearing chino pants and sport coats (except for the one woman in our party, who is wearing a black dress. A casual dress, but still a dress.) We are not decked out in our team shirts, complete with logos, numbers, advertisers, players' names. We are not wearing comically oversized floppy hats, team scarves. Our fingernails are clean. No tattoos, earrings, piercings, shaved or buzz- cut heads. No pale fleshy bellies hanging, exposed, over our belts. We are, after all, lawyers.

The rest of them, both Germans and Brits, are a sight. And they're loaded with booze. Bunched in the overcrowded, overheated subway car, Germans here, Brits there, each group eyeing the other, cautiously, hostile. Each group chanting their team chants, singing their team songs. Aimed like bullets at the opposition. It's too early for fights to break out, I tell myself, searching nevertheless for the as yet nonexistent Spanish police. Too early. It'll take another hour or two before these hooligans will begin to tear one another from limb to limb.

Then I realize what they are. They're clients waiting to happen.

The subway lets us out about a quarter of a mile from the stadium. The crowds are thick. Now I see the Spanish police. They're everywhere, decked out in full battle gear, helmets, batons, you name it. But I can quickly see they're not threatening. They smile when answering questions such as Where's the stadium?

And the stadium.

It's massive. Seats for 100,000. Total capacity 120,000 with standing room, which I'm told won't be permitted this evening. Security, you know, one of my companions says with the kind of British understatement I see on BBC TV shows. "A bit tepid, what?" some character will say to another as the two of them lie rotting in the hot box their captors have just placed them in for trying to escape from the prison camp. Before long, we and the rest of this sea of humanity arrive at the stadium. It is the Coliseum. Only twice the size, seating straight up and down all the way round.

We have great seats, a third of the way up, to the side of one of the goalposts. The evening is young. We have about an hour before game time. Night has not yet fallen. I notice that the German sections are on the opposite side of the stadium. There are about 20,000 to 30,000 Germans expected. More than 50,000 Brits. The rest Spaniards. But the numbers are off, my friends explain, because many of the tickets allotted to the Spanish have been scalped at very high prices. When issued, tickets cost £25 ($40). They've been scalped for as much as £200 to £300. That's simply too much of an incentive. So now the middle sections of the stadium, which were to have been a buffer zone of Spaniards between the Germans and English, are filled with randomly mixed seating of both Germans and English. Oh boy, I say to myself. Am I going to be in tomorrow's papers? "American Lawyer Injured/Assaulted/Maimed/Arrested at European Cup Final."

But then I notice something as the seats around us begin filling up with fans. There are two sides to these guys, all decked out in their logo'd red team soccer shirts, plastic cups of beer in their fists. Sure, they're working-class—laborers, many of them, by their looks. And they're prone to anger. But they're also Europeans, so they say Please, can I get by? as they make for their own seats, and thank you when you move. They smile at you and at one another. They exchange friendly greetings with obvious strangers. I get it. These fans are all family. They've come a great distance to Barcelona, at what must for them be a huge expense, to watch Man. U.—their team—take the treble. Same as the Germans. I begin to relax.

There's another forty minutes or so to go before the start of the game. Many of the seats around us are still empty. Where are the rest of the English fans? I ask my friend who's seated to my left. Still in the pubs, he jokes, as he nods over in the direction of the German sections across the way. Each German seat is filled. Not only that. Somehow, each seated German has a placard, which when raised in unison with the others helps spell out the initials of their team. That's fantastic, I think. Such orderliness, all these guys in their seats already, color-coordinated placards and all. But then I think, Sure, Germans. What do you expect? The British fans are still in the pubs swilling beer, while the Germans are already at the front line of this battle, ready for action. Stop it, I silently command myself. This is not 1939. Just then the seat to my right is occupied.

As he slides in next to me, his friend alongside him, the guy says hello. He's wearing all the red regalia of the other fans. Team shirt, the works. So is his friend, who also smiles hi to me. I say, Hi, how are ya? He hears an unfamiliar accent.

"You German, mate?" he asks, now no longer friendly.

"No," I say, "not German."

The guy turns away to chat with his friend, join in some of the team chants going on all around us. A minute or two later, he taps me on the arm. Not exactly a tap. But not exactly a punch either.

"You German?" he asks again.

"No, I'm not German," I repeat, this time pointedly, as if to signal, I wouldn't be caught dead being a German. Now the guy is stumped. He's heard a foreign accent. What the hell am I? Friend or foe? He stares at me suspiciously.

"Spanish?" he asks.

Now I'm frustrated. "No, not Spanish," I say. "Listen to me speak," I suggest, believing that all the world knows an American accent.

"Italian?" the guy asks.

Then I realize. This guy probably hasn't left his environs in his entire life. And here he is in Barcelona, Spain, to see his Man. U. go for the treble. I decide to help him.

"American," I say.

Actually, by now we are both shouting, the noise level in the stadium more than halfway along on its final journey to deafening. I can actually see the guy's eyes light up. He likes the idea of being seated next to an American. But then I see his eyes darken again. He looks me up and down. Suspicion has returned. Then he notices the people I'm with in the row of seats to my left, in their chinos and sport coats (with one black dress thrown in.) I get the stare again.

"We're lawyers," I say, with a meek smile and accompanying shrug. Like, you know, what can you do?

Bloody f__king hell, he says. (Actually, it comes out "bludie fookin'," with his strange kind of English accent.)

He puts his arm around me and gives me a little hug. "Like football, do ya, mate?" he shouts into my ear.

"Love it," I shout back, no fool I.

"You a Man. U. fan?" he shouts, adding that he himself is from Manchester.

You bet, I nod. "Bludie fookin' hell," he repeats, and then turns his attention to the chants and team songs erupting all around us.

This gives me an opportunity to turn to my friends seated in a line to my left. Have they seen my close encounter, I wonder. They're all smiling at me. They look like parents pleased that their little boy has found a new friend at the playground. Just then the announcer comes on, explaining that the opening festivities are about to begin. This takes a while to accomplish because everything has to be said in English, German, and Spanish.

A bunch of pom-pom girls run onto the field. Next some cheesy blowups of what to me look like plastic forest animals are inflated. And then believe it or not, a hugely overweight opera singer is wheeled out on a mini flatbed truck, singing an aria from Puccini. Opera, with these fans, I think. But the fans couldn't care less. To a man, they're all busy chanting their chants, singing their songs. The diva is superfluous, completely drowned out.

Now, a word about these chants and songs.

They're very clever, actually. The song lyrics are for the most part pegged to American show tunes. Like *Hello, Dolly!* Go figure. The words tell about a particular team player or the coach. They're intricate singing stories. All the fans know the words to all of them.

The chants are more primitive, more warlike. One is "Stand up for the champions, stand up." It comes out "Stind op fer the Champins, stind op." And you better, because everyone around you is motioning to the crowds to do as the chant commands. The English are singing and chanting. Across the way, the Germans are doing the same. God knows what the few Spaniards are doing. And then I hear the deafening roar telling me the teams have taken the field. The singing and chanting grows to fever pitch, the place now full of 100,000 frenzied fans. After a short warm-up period, some more multiple-language announcements, without much more, the game begins.

Now, unlike American football, soccer is played in two nonstop forty-five-minute periods, with a fifteen-minute halftime. Nothing stops the action. Nothing. Not even TV commercials. Millions of people across the globe are watching this on live TV and there are no commercials. Makes you understand why soccer doesn't catch on in the States, right? There's a digital clock on the scoreboards high atop each end of the stadium. But the time indicated is approximate only. The referees, or some other officials, keep the actual time, because some extra injury time is in fact allotted at the end of the game. This turns out to be critically important for this game, as you'll see.

Less than ten minutes into the game, one of the Manchester United players accidentally trips one of the Bayern Munich players. A foul is called. The Germans will get a free penalty kick at the goal. The crowd is on its feet, where, by the way, all 100,000 of us stay for most of the game. I watch as the Man. U. players form a defensive wall in front of their goal. The goalkeeper, who is the team captain, and indisputably one of the best goalies in the league, stands at the ready. No way anyone could penetrate this wall of stone. Then, the kick. The ball rises and flies right into the Man. U. goal. The fans around me groan. The goalkeeper falls to the ground, pounding his fists into the turf. The scoreboard registers 1–0. And then things get ugly.

The fans around me and, as far as I can tell, just about all of the 50,000 seated in our half of the stadium, explode. Invectives fly. Against the Germans, sure. Against the referees, sure. But the fans also turn on their own team. They curse them, scold them. Call them every dirty name in the book. They even curse their mothers. There's a lot of bludie fookin' this, bludie fookin' that. They are absolutely hateful. It's shocking. And all the while, interspersed with their threats and name calling, they're also singing and chanting their team on to victory. All this at a volume that would put most outdoor stadium rock concerts to shame. I feel dizzy, swept up in the middle of this frenzy. I look to my left, at my friends. They're quiet, clearly disappointed at Man. U.'s performance. One them sadly shakes his head at me. What a pity, he seems to be saying. Then I look to my right, at my new friend. He's actually crying. Tears are streaking down his unshaven face. And he's shouting invectives at his team, irately shaking his fist down at the field. He looks at me, then shouts something. What exactly, I can't hear. It's simply too noisy. But I don't need to hear. I can see his thoughts.

The rest of the first half remains scoreless. While Manchester United seems to be dominating the ball, keeping it downfield in German territory, they simply can't get anywhere near the Munich goal. The Germans are that good on defense. The Man. U. fans are by now nearly uncontrollable in their rage. If they could, I think they would storm the field, first to give their team a piece of their mind, and then to murder them. Spanish police have encircled the field, all of them helmeted, their backs to the game, carefully watching every one of us. Sometime just before halftime, I see this guy come in and take what had been the one empty seat in the row directly below me. He's a sight. Even by comparison.

He's young, very early twenties, I'd say. Fat, dirty; his hands and fingernails seem charred. He's shirtless, although he has what I suppose is a team flag draped over his flabby shoulders. His head is shaved, revealing what I think are burn marks from stubbing cigarettes out on his scalp. And he's wobbly beer drunk. Even the boys around him exchange glances with one another as he takes his seat in the row. Get a load of this bloke, they seem to be saying. I watch as Butt Head stands for a moment and then sits, slumped over with his filthy head in his hands as though he's going to be sick. He remains in that semi-comatose position for the rest of the game. The guy in the row directly below him glances back from time to time, clearly worried that Butt Head's going to puke down on his seat. His seat, if he happens to be standing at the time. On his head, if he isn't. Then the whistle blows, signaling halftime. That provides me with the opportunity for my second most interesting conversation with my new friend on the right.

"You bad luck, mate?" he asks, eyeing me suspiciously.

I can see the guy's clearly distraught. He's depressed. Not really himself. His team's losing. And he's searching for an explanation. One that's compatible with his religiously held view of his team's unequaled superiority over any other soccer team. It's got to be the bludie fookin' foreigner, he's thinking.

"I'm good luck," I say, with all the conviction I can muster, given that I'm shouting this out at the top of my lungs.

I look to my left. My friends are watching me again. Of course they can't hear a word of this. But their looks are clear. Isn't it nice how little Ronnie has made friends so quickly with some of the neighborhood children. No help from them, here. I take the bull by the horns. I grab my new friend by the shoulders. This isn't hard; I'm about a foot and a half taller than he is. I put my mouth as close to his left ear as I can stand it.

Then I shout, "I'm great luck, pal. With me here, Man. U. can't lose. Trust me," I urge, releasing my grip and then nodding assurance.

He continues to look at me suspiciously. You better be right, I think he's thinking. You better bludie fookin' be right. The whistle blows. It's time for the second half.

"Let's go! Man. U.!" I scream out, on my feet, my clenched fist raised in the air. Now I too have a stake in the outcome of the game.

But it doesn't look good for Manchester United. They play the entire second half much as they do the first. They dominate the ball, but they simply can't get near the goal. The crowd around me is beyond reason. They chant. They sing. They attack the German team. "Same old Germans. Always cheating," they scream over and over and over again. And, of course, they're hurling insults at their own team like rotten eggs from a bottomless basket. I see Butt Head. He's the only one at peace. If you call being so drunk you can't lift your head being at peace. I look to the clock. There's less than a minute to go. When the digits strike 45 minutes this game will be over. The Germans will have won the war, humiliating the

Brits in the process. I anxiously watch the clock, just a few seconds to go. I try and figure my way to the exit. Because it's going to be every man for himself. No way, I conclude. I'm going down with the ship. The clock shows 45. And then the most amazing thing happens.

The game is in injury overtime. No one, except the referees, apparently, knows exactly how much time is left. But whatever it is, it isn't much. A minute. Maybe two. I wonder if my friends will decide to leave. This game's over. Time to beat the crowds. The bloodshed. But this is soccer. No one leaves. Because anything can happen. And that night it does.

Manchester United gets the ball and then, as though there were nothing to it, the ball flies into the German goal. Amazing, I think. Here they've been trying to do this for ninety minutes, without even coming close, and then, easy as pie, they score. But so what? I think. Time's about to run out. What happens with a tie in a cup match, I wonder. And then, the ball's back in play. The Germans have it. The whistle's going to blow. Any second now. A Man. U. player steals the ball, dribbles to a teammate, then I see the ball defy gravity and fire itself once again into the German goal. The whistle does blow. The game's over. Manchester United has won the treble. Pandemonium erupts. There's one huge, collective roar. Then the English fans go absolutely insane with glee.

My new friend leaps into my arms and starts kissing me. We both fall backward across our seats. He rises, extends his hand to help me up. Once we're back on our feet, he loops one arm around me, the other around his mate, and together they start singing a team song as though it were "Rule, Britannia." And for them it was. I look down on the field. The Manchester United team is all huddled together, feverishly jumping up and down. And then I notice the German team. To a man, they are all lying prone on the ground, as though they're dead. And they stay in that position. Not one of them moves. They're absolutely destroyed. They're dead soldiers. I can't really tell what's going on across the stadium in the German section. But I can imagine.

This goes on for a while. My new friend won't let go of me. I'm his rabbit's foot. He keeps smiling at me. He's deliriously happy. So is everyone else around me. Even the guys I came with. They're simply overjoyed. Now they too are singing. The cup is presented in a short ceremony. The fans scream themselves hoarse. And then the most wonderful thing happens.

For almost the next hour the Manchester United team stays on the field, traveling to every section containing their fans. They wave to them, they jump up and down. They make it as clear as clear can be just how appreciative they are that these guys came all the way to Barcelona to root for them, to be here for them. They return all the love they're getting from their fans. No one seems to remember the invectives of the last ninety minutes. That's forgotten. Over. Man. U., their team, has won the treble.

Even Butt Head's on his feet. He's missed the entire game, but those around him have roused him, managed to convey to him that they've won. I watch him shake his head in disbelief, then turn, mouth fully open, to plant a kiss on the check of the guy next to him. Ugh! Then he pantomimes holding a beer can in his hand, lifting it repeatedly to his lips. Let's go get some beers, he seems to be saying. Then he turns and pukes onto the seat below him. I think I'm the only one who notices.

After a while my friends indicate that it's okay to leave. As we file out of the stadium, I say goodbye to my new friend. We hug. He says something. I can't hear what. Maybe he's telling me that the next time I'm in Manchester we should get together, maybe take in a game. We shake hands. I nod. Told you it'd be okay, I'm signaling. Never doubted you, mate, he nods back.

On the way out of the stadium, one of my companions buys me a team pennant. I keep it. Pack it in my suitcase for the trip home.

I'll need it next year when I'm in the U.K., in the stands, rooting for Man. U.

And it was better than court.

R.L.

A Trial Lawyer

I NOW CALL MYSELF A TRIAL LAWYER. THE UNFORTUNATE THING about *becoming* a trial lawyer is that one must start somewhere. One always has a first case—one hopes it is not like mine was.

I had been out of law school for about two years. As an associate, I was not given the opportunity to "hit the ground running"; rather, I quietly researched cases and prepared trials so that my boss, who, as you will learn, is a very kind and patient man, could actually try the cases. I was allowed to "second chair" many cases, but never actually got up and examined witnesses or spoke to the jury via argument, or otherwise. That is, until the *Jackson* case.

Our client was a young lady who was injured in a motor vehicle accident. She was riding as a passenger with her seat belt on. My boss thought there was no way anything could go wrong, so he let me try my hand at actually litigating a portion of the case.

Everything was going along great. I felt inspired. I felt like Matlock, and at times Perry Mason, and at times like both of them rolled up together. I was clever. I was witty. I was in control. Until a witness for the defense suddenly transformed herself before my eyes from an innocuous nuisance with little relevant testimony into a hostile b**** capable of sabotaging the entire case. I was devastated. Closing arguments were up next.

I began. I felt once again in control. I began with a summation of the testimony and told the jury why my client deserved a healthy amount of money in compensation for her injuries. When I got to the part about why the hostile witness was not to be believed, I became angry, frustrated, and to say the least, emotional. And then it happened. I felt a fountain of emotion wash over me. I stopped and turned my back to the jury. There was an American flag in front of me. I hung my head low. (Later, the judge would tell my boss that he thought I paused in a dramatic fashion and turned to the flag to make some point about the sanctity of our system of justice.) All of a sudden I burst into tears! My shoulders were bouncing up and down as I held my now-flooded face in my hands. My impassioned plea to the jury had turned into a crying jag.

I ran out of the courtroom and into a conference room and closed the door. My boss followed me in there within seconds.

"What's wrong?"

"I don't know."

"What happened?"

"I don't know."

I took several minutes to control myself and reentered the courtroom. When I did, the jury was sitting there—twelve stunned people looking at me as if to find a third eye in the middle of my forehead.

The judge excused the jury for a moment while it took up "house-keeping matters." The jury had no sooner left the courtroom when the defense lawyer rose to address the court.

"Your Honor, the defense moves for a mistrial."

"Granted."

All that work. All the preparation. All the money spent in preparation. Down the drain in a flash.

On the ride back home from the courthouse my boss discussed what happened to me as only he could. He did not ridicule me or appear disappointed in the least. Within twenty minutes, believe it or not, he had me laughing at myself. I'll never forget his kindness.

There are three P.S.'s to this story.

Within a month of this (mis)trial the judge had a heart attack and for some reason I wasn't all that sad. It's not that I didn't like him, but it helped to know that I wouldn't ever have to face him again.

The *Jackson* case settled out of court—within two weeks of the scheduled retrial.

My next two jury trials were sensational. Both of my next two juries awarded my clients more money than I requested.

I don't know what the secret of speaking to a jury is, but I suspect it has to do with believing so much in your client and in your client's cause that emotion begins to stir. I have now been a "trial lawyer" for seven years and I still get emotional at the closing argument stage of the trial.

Better Luck Next Time

My FIRST FELONY CASE AS A YOUNG LAWYER IN EASTERN Kentucky involved defending a man charged with attempted murder. I'll call him Bob.

It seems that Bob had a drinking problem. On the night in question Bob and his buddy purchased two gallons of Mogen David wine at a nearby package store. They spent the entire night drinking. The next morning Bob found himself sitting on his front porch with a .22 caliber rifle in his lap. His nephew came down the road toward his cabin and Bob opened fire. Fortunately, he missed.

After investigating the case, I determined that Bob had a defense to the charge. At the time of the shooting, Bob was still drunk. Blind drunk, in fact. My legal research indicated that Bob should be acquitted of the charge of murder (attempted murder, actually, since he somehow managed to miss his nephew), because he was too drunk to form the needed intent to commit murder.

On the day of trial, Bob was worried. The maximum sentence for attempted murder was five years in prison. Bob instructed me to meet with the prosecutor and see what kind of plea bargain I could get for him. After my meeting with the commonwealth attorney, I reported that if Bob would plead guilty as charged, the prosecutor would recommend to the court that Bob serve two years in jail. "I'll take it," Bob said, with a look of relief on his lined, unshaven face.

Now, as I said, I was a young lawyer, eager for the challenge of the courtroom. I thought we could beat the case and I very much wanted to try. I told Bob I thought we had a really good defense and just about begged him to let me take his case to the jury.

"That's just fine and dandy," Bob said, rubbing the stubble on his chin, all the while looking me up and down, apparently wondering how good—

or maybe marveling at how young—I was. "But are you gonna serve my time if I lose?"

Obviously, I couldn't promise him that. But I persisted, and finally Bob relented and let me take his case to trial. After a day of testimony, the jury bought our defense and returned a verdict of not guilty of attempted murder. He was convicted on the lesser charge of public drunkenness and was sentenced to thirty days in the local jail. Needless to say, Bob and I both were elated.

As the jury filed past us on their way out of the courtroom, Bob was busy vigorously shaking my hand. Then, just as most of the jurors were still within earshot, he congratulated me on my legal prowess and said, "The next time I shoot at that son of a bitch no good for nothin' nephew of mine, I won't miss."

I guess Bob thought I was a pretty good lawyer.

JOHN R. MCGINNIS
MCBRAYER, MCGINNIS, LESLIE & KIRKLAND
GREENUP, KENTUCKY

Sheep Thrills

I PRACTICED FOR MANY YEARS IN ALAMOSA, COLORADO, a small town in the southern part of the state. One day, several years ago, my partner and I were appointed to defend a man named Felipe Martinez, who had been charged in neighboring Costilla County with stealing a sheep.

After interviewing Felipe at some length, my partner and I could think of no defense, except possibly that Felipe was not smart enough to distinguish right from wrong—not insane, but just too dumb.

We went to talk to Costilla County's only doctor, Dr. Tozer, and told him the conclusion we had reached, and after some reflection, Dr. Tozer agreed with us. We asked him if he would testify to that effect, and he said he would.

After the prosecution rested, we put on Dr. Tozer as our only defense witness. We made our closing arguments. The jury retired, and relatively promptly returned a verdict of "not guilty." Upon hearing the verdict, Felipe, sitting at the counsel table with us, turned to us and asked, in a voice that could have been heard all the way back to Alamosa, "Does that mean I have to give the sheep back?"

RAPHAEL J. MOSES
ATTORNEY AT LAW
BOULDER, COLORADO

Go Figure

A NICELY DRESSED, WELL-SPOKEN, AFFABLE GENTLEMAN came to see me. It seems he had been criminally charged with passing bad checks. He acknowledged writing the checks in question, all of which had bounced. But he explained that the fault was not his. His bank had unfortunately lost one of his deposits, or possibly, he explained, applied his deposit erroneously to another customer's account. Consequently, when the merchants to whom he had written his checks tried to collect the funds, the bank would not honor payment.

It seemed like a plausible explanation. I agreed to take his case. The man was quite relieved that he now had a lawyer. Before leaving my office he provided me with a personal check for the modest retainer I had requested.

You guessed it.

The check bounced.

RICHARD V. BOSWELL
STONER, PRESTON & BOSWELL, CHARTERED
WESTMINSTER, MARYLAND

Do You Dig It?

THE CASE HAD GONE TO COURT. PLAINTIFF WON A JUDGMENT against defendant for money damages. So far so good. But defendant (now also a judgment debtor) never paid. So it was up to me as plaintiff's lawyer to use the power of legal process to find and seize defendant's assets, out of which plaintiff's judgment would be satisfied.

I had a subpoena issued for the judgment debtor, compelling him to give a deposition, where I would question him under oath as to where he had been hiding his assets. On the day of the deposition, I waited in vain. The debtor didn't show. So I went to court.

The judge issued an order requiring the debtor to appear in court and explain why he had not paid the judgment. I saw to it that the debtor was personally served with court's order. On the day of the hearing I waited in court. Again, the debtor didn't show.

This time the judge issued an arrest warrant. In standard legal language (habeas corpus ad subjiciendum) it ordered the sheriff to "bring the body before the court for further proceedings." A few days after the arrest warrant had been issued, I got a call from the debtor's wife. She was frantic. Choking back tears, she told me she would do whatever was necessary to fix this legal problem her husband had brought on himself. My client would be paid. "But," she asked, still sniffling, "do I have to dig him up?"

"Ma'am?" I asked.

"I read the warrant paper the sheriff left with me," she said. "Do I have to dig him up?"

It seems the judgment debtor had died just after the court's arrest warrant was issued.

It was tempting.

JOHN M. HODGES
HODGES, AVRUTIS & PRETSCHNER, P.A.
SARASOTA, FLORIDA

My First Case

MANY YEARS AGO AS A YOUNG LAWYER I LEARNED AN IMportant lesson that has stayed with me throughout my legal career.

My first case involved a man charged with breaking and entering. He was an employee of an important client of the law firm where I had just begun working, so there was a lot of pressure on me to win the case.

It seems that my client had been arrested while out on the street late at night in a neighborhood where there had been a series of burglaries. On the night in question, someone's house had been broken into during the approximate time my client was out on the street. The homeowner, who had accosted the burglar in his house, causing him to flee, positively identified my client as the man who had illegally entered his house.

My client's defense was that he had been at a birthday party in the neighborhood and had been sent out to buy more booze. At the time of trial, I somehow managed effectively to cross-examine the homeowner, casting some doubt on the accuracy of his identification of my client. I also produced about six people who testified that they had been at the party with my client and that he had left for the all-night liquor store too soon for him to have been the guy spotted at the house.

To my delight, the defendant was acquitted.

With a spring in my step I walked the few blocks from the courthouse to the building that housed my law firm and went right to the senior partner's office to share the good news. The man listened to me politely. Then, rather than congratulating me, he asked about the fee I had earned. "Fee?" I replied. I hadn't discussed a fee with my client. I figured that the firm would simply send him a bill for my services in the ordinary course. And that's when I received my lesson.

"Always remember," my senior partner instructed me, "representing defendants in a criminal case is like practicing the oldest profession in the world. Your services aren't worth a damn when the job is done!"

RALPH GEILICH
ATTORNEY AT LAW
MELBOURNE, FLORIDA

A Good Man

I'VE BEEN AN ATTORNEY FOR THIRTY-ONE YEARS WITH THE same law firm, specializing in estates and trusts. I love my work and love being a lawyer, despite the difficulties of the legal profession. While some may think my work somewhat dry and routine, I have found that every person and family to whom I have rendered professional services is different. From time to time I see the absolute best and worst that human nature has to offer.

I've probably drafted more than a thousand wills by now. It is true that some have been vindictive or attempts to "right wrongs" as perceived by the testator. Most of them, however, were motivated by the desire to take care of the human needs of loved ones after they had gone. And then there were those such as Walter S. Collin, who died leaving no one. His was the most memorable will I ever drafted.

Walter died in the early 1990s at age eighty-six. His wife, Hilde, died about eighteen months before him. They were childless and had no close relatives. He and his wife were European Jews who had come to America in 1938, just barely escaping the horrors of the Holocaust. Until his retirement, Walter spent his life working as a bookkeeper for a small business in the Buffalo area, living frugally and investing conservatively.

Hilde's will simply gave her entire estate to Walter. Walter gave much thought and attention to a new will after his wife's death and ultimately left his estate—about $2 million—to many persons who had befriended him and Hilde over the years, as well as to several local, national, and foreign charities that "did good work," as he put it.

Two of the more memorable provisions of Walter's will were:

1. A bequest of $25,000 to the National Gallery of Art, in Washington, D.C., "in gratitude to the United States of America for admitting my wife and me to such a nation at a time when our lives

were endangered." (Whenever I read about all the things that America is *not* as it approaches the millennium—not free enough, not equal enough, not this enough or that enough—I remember the gratitude and appreciation Walter and Hilde Collin expressed for what America *is.*)

2. A bequest of $12,500 for planting 2,500 trees in Israel. Walter and Hilde had never even traveled to Israel.

I may be privileged to draft several hundred more wills and handle the legal work for many more estates, but surely I won't forget Walter Collin's will and estate.

LAURENCE H. WOODWARD
MAGAVERN, MAGAVERN & GRIMM, L.L.P.
BUFFALO, NEW YORK

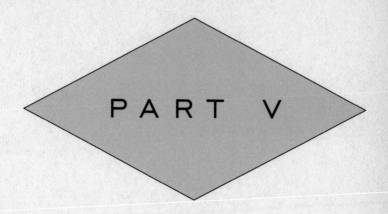

PART V

A WORD

WE LAWYERS MAKE OUR WAY WITH WORDS. IT'S THE PROVER-bial grist for our mill. Our careful, thoughtful way with words—when making our points, arguing our issues, convincing our judges and juries—is how we serve the interests of our clients. Doctors can mumble, salesmen can exaggerate, and politicians can—well, you know what they do with words. But the lawyer is the ultimate practitioner of the word. Who could be more careful in the use of words? It is with the greatest care that we choose what to say.

Of course, there are those times in lawyering when the word has escaped from its cage and run loose through the neighborhood. Sometimes it soils the neighbor's garden; more often it simply tires itself out and ultimately returns home.

Here are some stories where the word got loose.

How Often? . . . or *How?*

Central stage in a courtroom story is sometimes occupied by a lawyer, sometimes by a witness, and sometimes even by a judge. There is another presence in every courtroom, however—the court reporter—who almost never figures in the tale. This story, related to the undersigned by a court reporter, is the exception: here, a court reporter shares star billing with a familiar homonym.

The case being tried was a civil action for damages. Husband had fallen through a defective seat in a movie theater, and sought compensation for his injuries.

Although she had not been physically injured, Wife, too, was asserting a claim in the action—hers for "loss of consortium."

"Consortium," according to *Black's Law Dictionary,* is the "conjugal fellowship of husband and wife, and the right of each to the company, society, co-operation, affection, and aid of the other in *every* conjugal relation" (emphasis supplied).

The couple's attorney batted first, eliciting Husband's direct testimony with all of the delicacy possible under the circumstances.

"Without meaning to intrude unnecessarily into these, the most personal details of your private life, Mr. Doaks" (said the lawyer), "the law obliges me to inquire: How often did you engage in intimate relations with your wife prior to the unfortunate accident?"

"Oh, very often," said Husband, recalling with no little pride the man he used to be, prior to the unfortunate accident. "Really, quite often."

"While appreciating your natural reticence in discussing such matters, Mr. Doaks," the attorney persisted, gently, "might I ask you to be just a bit more specific?"

"Oh, we did it daily," recalled Husband, harking back wistfully to those salad days. "Sometimes twice a day."

"Yes," commiserated the attorney, moved yet again by his client's poignant story. "And how often do you engage in intimate relations with your wife *now, after* the unfortunate accident?"

"After the accident?" mused Husband. "After the accident . . . ?"

A fat pitch was about to be served up to the court reporter. He would be given one swing, and would not miss.

"Well . . . days can go by, now," Husband testified, ruefully. "Now we're lucky if we can manage it weekly."

"Excuse me, Your Honor," interrupted the court reporter. "How would the witness be spelling that?"

STEPHEN A. DVORKIN
DICKSTEIN SHAPIRO MORIN & OSHINKSY
NEW YORK, NEW YORK

Away with Words

An employee was recommended for dismissal by her supervisor. After numerous confrontations with her employer over an extended period of time, she came into my law office one day and told me, "Mr. Samuel, I need your help. They've put me through a lot. I have composed myself beautifully for all those years, but now I'm decomposed."

LARRY SAMUEL
RITTENBERG AND SAMUEL, L.L.C.
NEW ORLEANS, LOUISIANA

A Blessed Event

IN MY FIRST JURY TRIAL I DEFENDED A MAN ACCUSED IN A PA-ternity suit. We lost. The jury returned a verdict holding him responsible. What could I do?

I turned to my client and congratulated him on becoming a father.

WALTER W. SNELL
SNELL & SNELL
DAYTONA BEACH, FLORIDA

Justice Triumphed!

[Editor's Note: Here is another story that has become a part of lawyer folklore.]

A FATHER-AND-SON CRIMINAL DEFENSE TEAM WERE REPRE-senting a despicable person, against whom the evidence of guilt was overwhelmingly strong. The father, the more mature and experienced member of the team, participated in the first half of the trial and then, because of a scheduling conflict, left to try another case in another city. The son was advised to do the best he could under the circumstances and report the expected result when the jury returned its verdict.

A day or two later the father received a fax from his son and it simply said, "Justice triumphed!" (The son in his excitement had neglected to advise his father that the jury had unexpectedly and miraculously acquitted their client.)

The father's return fax was equally terse: "Appeal at once!"

Lawyer Howe

A<small>FTER MY FATHER</small>, G<small>EDNEY</small> M. H<small>OWE</small>, J<small>R</small>., <small>DIED, WE PUT TO-</small>gether a book of stories he used to tell about lawyering in our South Carolina town back in his days. The two that follow are among my favorites.

They Call It Embezzlement

I remember hearing Gedney explain the different treatment afforded to people who were charged with stealing. According to Gedney, back in the earlier days when it was not mandatory for everybody to have a lawyer, a man who was charged with stealing five dollars would no doubt be hustled into the courtroom from the detention cell, he would appear without a lawyer, and the clerk would say to him, "Well, what do you want to do? Plead guilty or go to trial and if you get convicted have the judge be tough on you?" And, of course, the defendant would plead guilty.

According to Lawyer Howe, if a guy was charged with stealing fifty dollars, he might be out on bond and he might be sitting out in the audience and when his case was called, he thus might come to the bar without having people shoving him and almost physically mistreating him, and they would show him some degree of deference and he would be permitted to plead guilty, and the judge would give him a sentence, probably not so harsh as the one he had just given to the fellow for stealing five dollars.

And according to Lawyer Howe, if the guy was charged with stealing five hundred dollars, he no doubt would not only be out on bond and seated out in the audience, but when he came to the bar he would have a lawyer with him, and he would receive a sentence, probably not so tough as the two earlier sentences.

And if a man was charged with stealing five thousand dollars, he would, of course, be out on bond, be seated out in the audience, and be represented by a lawyer, and you know, a pretty good lawyer, and as a consequence thereof, he no doubt would be put on probation.

A fellow charged with stealing fifty thousand dollars would no doubt be represented by two or three lawyers, one of them probably a state senator, and he'd, of course, be out on bond, be seated out in the audience, he'd of course have character witnesses to come and speak for him, and, according to Lawyer Howe, the function of the character witness is to pave the way for the man's return to society, because it's a foregone fact that he is going to be returned to society because he's going to be put on probation. The story told by the character witness normally has something to do with the fact that the man took the money because he had a brother who was in trouble, or some other story that is designed to show that taking it was really some noble gesture on the part of the defendant, and certainly was not done for his own benefit.

And then, Lawyer Howe said, if the amount involved is five hundred thousand dollars, they don't even call it stealing; they call it embezzlement.

KERMIT KING

More Money for Hooper

It seems that in the town of Poordunk, Texas, the cows would graze on the railroad track and every month the train would run over and kill the best bull in the herd. A small-town lawyer in this town, which was the county seat, would file a suit for a hundred dollars in Magistrate's Court, which was the maximum amount that could be sued for in that court.

Hoover Hooper, a wealthy Harvard graduate, who was the attorney for all the railroads in Texas, would ride down from Dallas in his chauffeur-driven Cadillac to this dusty little town of Poordunk and park in front of the town's only store, where the magistrate held court, and the case would be tried before a six-man jury.

Hooper would explain to the magistrate and the jury that the law did not hold the railroad responsible for an unfenced bull that would roam upon the railroad track, but the lawyer for the owner would merely say, "The railroad killed the bull and it has a lot of money to pay for it." So the jury would go out and in less than one minute come back with the full verdict of a hundred dollars for the owner of the dead bull against the railroad.

After this happened three times in a row, Old Hooper said to himself that he would have to figure out some way to stop the jury from finding a verdict against the railroad, even though the verdict was much less than the expense of going from Dallas to Poordunk. So at the next trial, the lawyer for the owner of the dead bull made his usual argument and then Old Hooper got up, and he addressed the jury while twirling his flashy gold watch chain that had a large diamond appended thereto as follows:

"Gentlemen of the jury, my name is Hoover Hooper and I, of course, am not one of your local yokels, but hail from the big city of Dallas. You might wonder why a big-city lawyer like me is down here trying a mere cow case. Well, I'll tell you, it's not because I think I'll win this case before you. It's because of the money I'll make. As a matter of fact, none of you has the sense to find for the railroad, and even if you did, you wouldn't find against your neighbor, even though he is clearly wrong and his cow was on our tracks. But don't think you'll make me mad when you bring in a verdict in favor of your neighbor, because all that verdict will mean to me is MORE MONEY FOR HOOPER.

"I'll promptly appeal to the county judge, who is elected by ignorant yokels like you whom he does not want to offend, so he will surely affirm your verdict. But all that means is just MORE MONEY FOR HOOPER.

"For then, I shall appeal to the Circuit Court, where the judge, like the county judge, owes his job to the votes of yokels such as you. So he too will probably affirm your verdict. And that will mean MORE MONEY FOR HOOPER.

"From there I'll go to the Court of Appeals, and should it affirm your verdict, it only means just that MUCH MORE MONEY FOR HOOPER.

"For I shall appeal to the Supreme Court, which is appointed and which surely will have the intelligence you do not have and will promptly decide the case in favor of the railroad, which you yourselves would do, but for your ignorance. But I am thankful for your ignorance, because it just means MORE MONEY FOR HOOPER."

The jury went out this time and in less than one minute it returned with a verdict for the railroad. The lawyer for the owner of the dead bull was shocked and blurted out, "How could you do that?" The foreman, as quick as a jackrabbit, replied, "We ain't gonna let that old S.O.B. Hooper make any more money."

J. C. HARE
THOMAS P. BUSSEY
T. ALLEN LEGARE

GEDNEY M. HOWE, III
ATTORNEY AT LAW
CHARLESTON, SOUTH CAROLINA

Think Before You Speak

I HAD A CASE IN MOBILE, ALABAMA, A FEW YEARS BACK IN-
volving a claim of theft of trade secrets. One of the witnesses who had to
provide a deposition to the plaintiff's lawyer was an engineer employed by
my client. We lawyers take quite seriously the need to prepare our witnesses before they give testimony, either at trial or by deposition before
trial. So I met with the engineer before his deposition and gave him my
standard advice about answering questions at a deposition. My advice
went more or less like this:

"Since we will be in a conference room at a lawyer's office—as opposed to a courtroom, where a judge and jury would be present to watch
you answer—take all the time you need before answering any question.
Think about *every* question carefully before you answer it. Remember that
the deposition transcript will show only your answer, and not how long it
took you to answer. So be very careful and take time before providing your
answers to opposing counsel's questions."

The deposition began with the usual "Please state your name for the
record." A full minute later the witness gave his name. "Your address?"
Another full minute and then an answer. And so it went. At the time of the
first break, after about an hour, the questioning had not progressed beyond the witness's educational background. At this rate we wouldn't be
getting to the facts of the case until late in the afternoon, if not the next
day. As we left the conference room, the plaintiff's lawyer asked if he
could speak to me alone. I was sure he was about to scold me for over-
preparing the witness. Instead, once we were alone he asked me in all sin-
cerity, "So the poor guy suffers from narcolepsy, doesn't he?"

KENNETH S. GOODSMITH
GOODSMITH, GREGG & UNRUH
CHICAGO, ILLINOIS

It's All Greek to Me

I REPRESENT CO-OP AND CONDOMINIUM ASSOCIATIONS THROUGH-out New York City. In that capacity I deal with many of the city's well-heeled and sophisticated residents.

A few years ago, while my office was undergoing heating repairs, I was meeting with a group of condominium board members to dissuade them from resigning their thankless task. I warned them that Aristotle once said, "Those who consider themselves too wise to govern are destined to be ruled by fools."

Upon hearing that, the steamfitter sitting on my floor in a sweaty T-shirt and a reversed baseball cap, fixing the pipes, looked up from his torch, grinning eyes shining through his soot-covered face, and said, "That was Socrates."

And I think it was.

ELLIOTT MEISEL
BRILL & MEISEL
NEW YORK, NEW YORK

The Meat of the Matter

My FIRST JOB AS A LAWYER WAS WITH A SMALL FIRM IN THE outback of Australia. My boss, Terry, was representing a local cattle rancher in litigation over the questionable pedigree of some head of cattle the rancher had recently purchased. It was to be a two-day trial, and our client's spouse, a no-nonsense rancher's wife, had come to court to watch the proceedings for the day. Terry was somewhat renowned for his verbosity, and the trial, which was being held in an un-airconditioned courtroom in the savage Australian summer, soon dragged into the afternoon with little progress. This was much to the increasing frustration of our client's wife, who, quite clearly, wanted the whole thing to be over with as soon as possible.

When the proceedings mercifully closed for the day, we were invited out to our client's ranch for dinner. No sooner had we sat down to a hearty meal of steak and vegetables than the rancher was called outside to assist in the difficult birth of a calf.

"Perhaps you can come with me," the rancher asked my boss. "I'll show you how to deliver the bull."

"Good idea," replied the rancher's wife laconically to her husband. "And perhaps when you go to court with Terry tomorrow, he can return the favor."

COLIN FLANNERY
OFFICE OF LEGAL COUNSEL
SCHLUMBERGER INDUSTRIES, INC.
NORCROSS, GEORGIA

Disorder in the Court VI

QUESTION: Now, Mrs. Marsh, your complaint alleges that you have had problems with concentration since the accident. Does that condition continue today?

ANSWER: No, not really. I take a stool softener now.

QUESTION: And what did you see when [the accused] pulled down his pants?

ANSWER: It looked like a penis, only smaller.

QUESTION: Do you recall whether you had discussions about your concerns?

ANSWER: Did I discuss these concerns, or did I discuss my concern about the concern that I would be fired if I objected too much?

ANSWER: I guess your concerns about raising these concerns. Whether you ever discussed that you were concerned about raising these concerns, if you were so concerned.

QUESTION: What did you do to prevent the accident?

ANSWER: I just closed my eyes and screamed as loud as I could.

QUESTION: Where were you?

ANSWER: I was in the front right passenger seat.

QUESTION: What state were you in?

ANSWER: I was slightly inebriated. I was in good spirits—

QUESTION: Were you in Illinois?

ANSWER: I have absolutely, positively no regard for the medical profession, and you may center that, underline it, and dot and dash it. I despise them; I loathe them; I detest them; I find them the scum of the earth. Other than that, I have no problem with them.

QUESTION: What happened then?

ANSWER: He told me, he says, "I have to kill you because you can identify me."

QUESTION: Did he kill you?

ANSWER: No.

QUESTION: Are you married, sir?

ANSWER: Yes.

QUESTION: And to whom are you married?

ANSWER: My wife.

QUESTION: Please put an *X* where you fell.

ANSWER: On my behind?

QUESTION: No, I meant on the exhibit.

ANSWER: I told my attorney I would take a polyester test to show I wasn't lying, but no one ever gave me one.

Give It to Me Straight

AN ELDERLY PARTNER OF MINE, ON THE VERGE OF RETIRE-
ment, got a call from a Japanese lawyer he had known years before. This
lawyer had, thirty-some years earlier, served briefly as the legal officer in
the Japanese Embassy in Washington, D.C. The two lawyers had kept in
touch over the years, exchanging birthday cards and visiting each other occasionally. The Japanese lawyer had called because he had some legal
business to refer to our firm. It seems that a Tokyo-based corporation had
been placed under investigation by the U.S. Department of Justice for allegedly violating U.S. laws in connection with the manufacture and sale of
some of its products.

So off to Tokyo we went—my elder partner, one of our junior partners, and I.

The corporate conference room we were escorted into that first
morning after our arrival was large, too large I thought, as I greeted a
line of Japanese men (no women) standing precisely shoulder to shoulder, waiting to greet and bow as we were introduced. There were the
chairman of the company, about the same age as my elder partner, and
then, in descending order, a number of drably suited corporate executives ranging from their apparent sixties downward, the last one looking
to be about mid-forties. At the other end of the room were two translators, younger men, standing at the ready with pens and steno pads.
Standing alongside them was the Japanese lawyer who had called us in
on the case.

The conference table was massive. We were shown to one side. The
chairman and his boys took the other, while the two translators sat at the
far end. The Japanese lawyer walked to our side and bowed respectfully
while saying something in Japanese to the already seated chairman. I
don't understand Japanese, but it seemed as though he was asking the
chairman, "Okay with you, I sit over here with these guys?" The chairman

grunted a short response, following which the Japanese lawyer bowed again, then took a seat on our side of the table.

The meeting began with the chairman making a welcoming speech (he would stop after each sentence for the translators to translate), which was more befitting a visiting head of state than a bunch of lawyers here to try and fix a problem. I also noticed by the way that each of the corporate executives watched and listened to the translators that they could speak English. How well I couldn't tell, but they could speak English all right. I could see it. These guys are very careful, I remember thinking. They don't want to miss a nuance, a word or phrase that we say. That's why the two translators.

When the chairman's welcoming speech finally ended, he looked at us. It was clearly time for us to reciprocate. My elder partner cleared his throat.

Now, a word about my elder partner. I mentioned that he was on the verge of retirement. (He actually stayed on with the firm for a few more years after this trip.) I had been given to understand that in his day he was quite an effective lawyer. Whether it was age, or the succession of wives who had passed through his life, each taking with her a rather significant share of his net worth, or something else, I don't know, but he was what one would politely call a bit out of touch with things.

His speech began with a recollection of the first time he saw Tokyo— as a young bomber pilot during World War II. He reminisced at some length about his success in turning the streets and neighborhoods of Tokyo to rubble. As he spoke he smiled affectionately across the table, nodding with appreciation at how effective he and the rest of the Army Air Corps had been in their destructive war effort. At one point in his remarks he paused, about to refer to the Japanese with that unfortunate name that was so popular with Americans in the 1940s. Thank goodness, he let that one go. Instead he asked the chairman—seeing as how they were about the same age, he remarked—what he did during the war. He said this as though he were discussing some intramural sporting event in which we and the Japanese had jointly engaged.

The chairman glared at him, then let forth with a barked barrage of words. (This time not waiting for the translators at all.) As I sat there stunned, listening, I couldn't help but think of the scene in the movie *The Bridge on the River Kwai* where the Japanese prison camp commandant (was that Sessue Hayakawa?) gives a tongue-lashing to Alec Guinness, who plays the ranking British officer in the prison camp. Of course, the movie was in English and what was occurring before me was in Japanese. Still, the similarity was clear enough. I was standing inside the prison compound, under that horrible tropical sun, dressed in my sweat-soaked khaki uniform, watching as our senior officer was being subjected to this terrible tirade from Colonel Saito (Hayakawa's character). All the while my elder partner sat there with a serendipitous smile on his face, pleasantly listening as the chairman ranted across the table.

When the chairman finally finished, his eyes shot to the translators. The one who had been writing all of this down looked up from his notes with clear terror in his eyes. What? You serious? Say that? Now? his eyes were clearly asking.

"Holy shit." (That was my junior partner mumbling under his breath. While I kept silent, I certainly shared his sentiments.)

The chairman barked more Japanese at the translator. Yes! Now! You worthless dog! (As far as I was concerned, no translation was necessary.)

The translator shrugged. Here goes, his body seemed to be saying as he looked down at his notes and was about to speak. Just then, the Japanese lawyer held his hand out to the translator, indicating that he should hold up a moment. Then, while still seated, with a deep, respectful bow, he spoke to the chairman, all the while keeping his eyes focused on the table in front of him.

"He's pleading for our lives," my junior partner whispered to no one in particular.

Boy, was the chairman pissed. He didn't even let the Japanese lawyer finish before again ordering the translator to translate. (No English version of what was happening was necessary here.) But the Japanese lawyer again held his hand to the translator and with a second, even deeper bow across the table to the chairman, he tried once more. And so it went, back and forth, until the Japanese lawyer finally wore the chairman down. The chairman waved his hand in the air dismissively. (All right, okay, he was saying. What the hell.) Then the Japanese lawyer turned to us with a pleasant smile and said, "Translator will translate," as though nothing out of the ordinary had just happened. He said a few curt words in the direction of the translator, all the while still smiling in our direction.

My elder partner turned his attention down to the end of the table as the translator studied the voluminous notes he had taken of the chairman's retort.

"Drove a truck," was all the translator said of the chairman's war ef-fort. He looked up from his notes. Yeah, right! the twinkle in the transla-tor's eyes said.

"Ah!" my elder partner said, with appreciation, nodding pleasantly at the now stonefaced chairman.

"Discuss case," the Japanese lawyer quickly said to me in an obvious attempt to extricate us from the brink of World War III. I swear I couldn't see his lips move.

So I began a discussion of the case. Now, these cases are very compli-cated. We lawyers spend a lot of time dancing around issues and whatnot with our clients. We kind of sneak up on the facts—on what really hap-pened. We talk about theories and probabilities, and what the other side (here the U.S. Department of Justice) might *attempt* to prove and so on. We ask indirect questions, we muse about what perhaps might have oc-curred or how the other side might interpret what might have occurred. The process takes a while, even without translators. But eventually, the lawyers come to an understanding of the strengths and weaknesses of their client's case. And it's done in such a way that the client sees the lawyer trying to understand the case and to help without actually requir-ing the client to confess to anything embarrassing, or (heaven forbid) illegal.

We were going along swimmingly, the two translators working, the conversation across the table in full swing, the pieces of the puzzle begin-ning to fall into place, when my elder partner spoke again.

"Might I just ask a question?" he said to the chairman.

"Bombs away," my junior partner said in a stage whisper. (I didn't think he was being too helpful here.)

The chairman looked in the direction of my elder partner, who cleared his throat again, then spoke.

"Did you do it?" he asked. The room went silent. The place turned into a vacuum. For a moment no one spoke. The translators stared at my elder partner, along with all the other folks in the room. Now, I mentioned that I thought all the Japanese in the room spoke English; yet, to a man, they all turned toward the translators. Maybe they collectively believed they had misheard the question. And here we were going along so well, I remember thinking.

One of the translators bowed in the direction of the chairman and spoke something before looking down at his notes and repeating my elder partner's question in Japanese. Now, remember, boss, I think he said. I'm only translating here. It ain't me who's asking this.

"No, I mean," my elder partner continued after the translation, "did you do it?" You know, like his question wasn't clear enough first time around.

The chairman spoke to the Japanese lawyer. My junior partner, again in a stage whisper, said, "He's asking what's the English word for bozo." I gave him a look. He shrugged. Come on, lighten up, his shrug said. We're all gonna die anyway.

The Japanese lawyer and the chairman embarked on another long discussion, after which the chairman turned to my elder partner and spoke. He then turned to the translator and nodded for him to repeat what he had just said in English.

"Let's eat lunch," the translator said, his face buried in his notes.

And we did.

Believe it or not, I think we actually did a good job for our Japanese client. It took a while, but I believe we managed to extricate them from their U.S. legal problems.

After our first trip to Japan, it was decided that our elder partner's greatest contribution would come from any further thoughts he might have while sitting at his desk in Washington, D.C.

He actually made a very gracious speech at the dinner our client hosted in Washington after the case was over.

R.L.

Seeing It All

I**F YOU PRACTICE LAW LONG ENOUGH, EVENTUALLY YOU'LL SEE**
it all.

What?

My partner tried a complicated product-liability case for several days and
lost. He filed a motion for a new trial. The court granted his motion.

Opposing counsel filed an appeal and requested a transcript of the
trial proceedings. More than the usual delays occurred in getting the typed
transcript of testimony from the court reporter. After an interminable
time with no transcript, the story finally broke. There would be no transcript.

It turns out the court reporter was deaf.

The court reporter had been pretending the whole time. He was wig-
gling his fingers over his stenographic machine for the duration of the entire trial, with a "backup" tape recorder actually recording the testimony.
When something happened to the tapes, all record of the trial disappeared.

After much moaning and gnashing of teeth (and threats of suit against
the court reporter) by the other side, the case went to trial again with a different court reporter. Fortunately for the first court reporter, my partner
lost the retrial.

No harm, no foul.

All Balled Up

Ralph was the classic "innocent bystander," who was shot in the groin by
the police while watching a gunfight between cops and robbers. Ralph
came to me, and I filed suit against the police for reckless use of firearms.

In preparing my client for his deposition, I cautioned him that street talk and slang might be misunderstood. (He was prepared, understandably, to testify that he had been shot in the balls.) We went over the appropriate medical testimony.

At his deposition, everything was proceeding uneventfully until Ralph was asked where he had been shot. Ralph became very quiet and stared intently at the ceiling for an unusually long time. Clearly, he was searching for the right word. Then he got it. Ralph brightened, smiled, and spoke in a clear and unambiguous voice.

"They got me in the technicals."

The other lawyer nodded understandingly, then moved to his next question.

Ralph beamed at me, obviously pleased that he had followed my advice.

The Missing Witness

My partner was representing a man who was injured while skating at a roller rink.

Throughout the case, he tried unsuccessfully to find the former roller rink guard, who was the only eyewitness to the injury.

When the case was called to trial, the jury was selected without the presence of his client, who was coming from out of town.

The next morning, our client arrived at the courtroom and happily congratulated my partner for finding the missing eyewitness. In response to my partner's incoherent grunts of confusion, our client pointed to the jury box. The former roller rink guard was one of the jurors.

A mistrial was promptly granted.

RICHARD H. WILLITS, P.A.
LAKE WORTH, FLORIDA

Faking It

I WAS APPOINTED BY THE COURT TO REPRESENT RAPHAEL Sanchez, a rather striking-looking transvestite, who had been picked up on an outstanding arrest warrant.

Do you know what you've been charged with? I asked my new client.

Counterfeiting, he/she said.

Well, there you go.

JOHN L. MACHADO
BALDWIN, MOLINA, ESCOTO & MACHADO, P.C.
WASHINGTON, D.C.

I Can See Clearly Now

For many years our law office had a very wonderful and vivacious but verbally challenged receptionist. Her name was Johna.

I had been representing a young man injured in an automobile accident. Following his meeting with his doctor, he called me to advise of his injuries. I was out of the office, so he asked our receptionist to tell me that he had been x-rayed and the doctor diagnosed two herniated disks and a fracture. The doctor intended to place him on permanent disability. Johna left me the following message:

```
To  Dennis
Date  12/2        Time  11:34    A.M. ☐
                                 P.M. ☐

      WHILE YOU WERE OUT
M   Dan Morin
of
Phone
      Area Code        Number        Extension

TELEPHONED        ✓   PLEASE CALL
CALLED TO SEE YOU     WILL CALL AGAIN
WANTS TO SEE YOU
RETURNED YOUR CALL    URGENT

Message
   Dr. Lahey is putting
   him on permanent
   visibility

   2 discs + a fraction
              Operator
```

Dennis E. Lind
Datsopoulos, MacDonald & Lind, P.C.
Missoula, Montana

A Dog of a Case, or, Only in America

My client James Bond (his real name, honest) was sued by one Margaret Matthews in the Magistrate Court of Johnson County, Kansas. Ms. Matthews claimed in her suit that her dog Choo Choo, while on a leash, was attacked by James Bond's dog, Nugget. As a result she sought a judgment for damages for medical expenses and injuries suffered by Choo Choo.

As defense counsel we carefully investigated the incident. We then filed the following responsive pleading contesting liability. (I have deleted the more technical portions of our pleading.)

IN THE MAGISTRATE COURT OF JOHNSON COUNTY, KANSAS

MARGARET MATTEWS,
Plaintiff

Vs.	No. 26828
	Div. III

JAMES BOND,
Defendant.

ANSWER OF DEFENDANT

Comes now the defendant, and for his answer to the petition of the plaintiff alleges and states as follows:

1. [Deleted]

2. [Deleted]

3. That the dispute arose as a result of Choo Choo's deliberate trespass upon the premises of defendant, over which Nugget presides and the protection of which is his responsibility; that Choo Choo was demonstrably pugnacious during the course of said trespass and further gave indication of his intent to defile Nugget's domicile, and that Nugget's actions were reasonable in light of the obvious malicious intent of Choo Choo.

4. That at the time of the affray, Choo Choo was in fact wearing a leash, as alleged, but the controlling end of same was unoccupied and it was therefore dragging behind him, all in violation of the ordinances of the City of Overland Park, Kansas.

5. That the coup de grâce, if any, was delivered not at the residence of Choo Choo, as alleged, but at a vacant lot across the street from Nugget's home; that the court should take judicial notice of the fact that among schoolboys and dogs the traditional forum for resolving differences of opinion in an extra-legal manner is a vacant lot and that the location is therefore irrelevant as it relates to fault.

6. That while defendant is certain that Nugget could have seriously injured Choo Choo had he wanted to do so, by reason of his gentle nature he simply impressed upon Choo Choo the error of his ways in a manner calculated to impress itself on a nonreasoning being; Nugget did not chew Choo Choo.

7. That while Choo Choo is in all probability a boon companion to plaintiff, and considered one of the family, his genetic makeup is such as to render unavailable to him the relief granted a human sufferer of personal injuries.

8. That if the foregoing does not accurately state the laws of Kansas, defendant asserts in the alternative that Choo Choo is the proper party to this action and that it should have been brought by plaintiff in his behalf as his next friend.

9. That if plaintiff's cause of action is predicated upon the negligence of defendant, the petition fails to make clear what that negligence was; that Nugget's negligence would not be imputable to defendant since the said Nugget is not a reasonable and prudent man, whatever his qualities as a dog, and could therefore not be guilty of negligence.

10. That if the foregoing does not accurately state the laws of Kansas, defendant asserts in the alternative that Choo Choo was guilty of contributory negligence and that said contributory negligence would likewise be imputed to plaintiff; that in addition, plaintiff was guilty of contributory negligence by permitting Choo Choo to run loose with no supervision; in support of his contention, defendant offers the following Ode to the Law on Choo Choo:

> If Choo Choo plaintiff,
> Would protect from pain
> Why did not plaintiff
> Choo Choo train?

11. That by reason of Nugget's being a German Shepherd and Choo Choo's being a Poodle, it is a clear case of res ipsa loquitur as to Choo Choo's assumption of the risk in engaging Nugget in physical battle.

WHEREFORE, defendant prays that plaintiff take naught by her petition herein and that all costs herein be taxed to said plaintiff.

The case was dismissed.

JOE L. NORTON
NORTON HUBBARD RUZICKA & KREAMER L.C.
OLATHE, KANSAS

Getting It Backwards

PLAINTIFF WAS A SEVENTY-YEAR-OLD MAN WHO SUED AN AUTO-mobile repair shop for negligence. At trial plaintiff testified that his daughter gave him a 1982 Volvo that had approximately 250,000 miles. He took the car to the defendant's shop and asked what it needed. Defendant sold plaintiff new tires, shocks, and struts. After the repairs plaintiff complained that the car rode too stiff. Defendant offered to refund plaintiff's money if he returned the parts. Plaintiff sued instead.

At trial plaintiff described all the problems with the way the car rode after the repairs. He described how "smooth" and "fine" the car rode before defendant did the work. Then his lawyer asked him about the tires.

Q. Mr._____, did you purchase four new tires from defendant?
A. Yes, sir.
Q. Did defendant properly install the tires?
A. No, they did not. They installed them tires backwards.
Q. How did you learn the tires were installed backwards?
A. When I went back the following year the repairman told me the tires had to be rotated.

JAMES C. AYERS, JR.
CLARK & SCOTT, P.C.
BIRMINGHAM, ALABAMA

Right Church, Wrong Pew

In THE PRACTICE OF IMMIGRATION LAW, LANGUAGE DIFFER-ences sometimes create misunderstandings even with the most English-fluent client. Years ago an erudite Middle Eastern gentleman consulted me on his prospects for immigration. He sat in my office very poised and gentle in demeanor with eyelids relaxed at half-mast. I explained that his learnedness and occupation suggested him to be an excellent candidate for immigration in the national interest. His current nonimmigrant visa status was running out, though, so I counseled, "It will be necessary for you first to return to your home country in order then to immigrate properly to the U.S."

"Ah, but I have political difficulties in the homeland. That is why I came here. I cannot go back."

Asylum seemed his only route, a difficult route not readily recommended. In an effort to make my client understand the difficulty of this choice I relied on a worn analogy. "Seems you are between a rock and a hard place."

His eyelids shot up. "But I'm not from Iraq, I'm from Iran!" he exclaimed.

MARGARET MAKAR
ATTORNEY AT LAW
DENVER, COLORADO

Duh

A FRIEND OF MINE WHO WAS A CIRCUIT COURT JUDGE IN FORT Lauderdale, Florida, presided over a not so very complicated personal injury case. It seems the plaintiff, who was in an automobile accident, was somehow claiming a disease unrelated to the accident. He sued the opposing driver.

The young lawyer who represented the plaintiff was very inexperienced. As a result he did his best to make a simple case as complicated as possible. Jury selection took three days. The young advocate wanted to read a list of five hundred diseases to each prospective juror, not one of which his client had. He asked the judge to permit him to read to the jury the obituary of Joe Louis and an unknown man in Tamarac, Florida, because each of them had died of some diseases on the list.

Finally, with the judge's gentle prodding, the trial got under way. After a dramatic—and long—opening statement, the young lawyer called his first witness, a board-certified neurologist and neuro-biomechanical engineer. His apparent purpose in calling an expert as his first witness was to impress the jury with sufficient medical testimony so that they would be persuaded that his client was suffering an illness caused by the accident.

For over an hour, the lawyer went over the expert's qualifications: his schooling, his advanced degrees, his scholarly writings, his various professorships, and other teaching positions. On and on it went. Finally, satisfied that he had now shown the jury that this first witness was not only the most expert medical professional in his fields, but one of the smartest persons ever to have walked the face of the earth as well, he asked his first real question.

"Doctor," the young lawyer asked his witness, "what would you say is the most complex structure known to man?"

Expecting a two-word answer ("the brain"), the lawyer turned and, with a triumphant smile, squarely faced the jury.

The expert witness pondered the question with all the solemnity and deep thought the occasion required. Then he rubbed his thick dark beard and pondered the ceiling. Finally, he turned to the jury and with a knowing smile, he replied.

"It's the Sears Tower in Chicago, I think."

Defense verdict in five minutes.

G. WARE CORNELL, JR., P.A.
FORT LAUDERDALE, FLORIDA

Smell's Bells

Y EARS AGO, I EMPLOYED A YOUNG LAWYER WHOM I CAREFULLY trained in the ins and outs of trial practice. There are many practical things not taught in law school that you need to know when actually trying cases in court. One of those things is when—and, more important, how—to move for a mistrial.

There are times when what is said in court is so prejudicial to your client that, once the jury has heard the evidence in question, it is simply too late for the judge to correct the problem. Judges generally don't like to grant motions for mistrial, because when they do, the trial has to start over again from the very beginning. A new jury has to be selected, opening statements must be made again, and so on. Judges like to move their dockets and dispose of their cases the first time around. So they like to believe that by giving the jury what they call a cautionary instruction—"Ladies and gentlemen of the jury, I want you to disregard what you just heard, as though you never heard it, and let's move on to some other evidence"— the problem has been solved. But as they say, you can't unring a bell.

Over several months, I spent considerable time training this young lawyer in the practical aspects of trial lawyering. When we came to the subject of mistrials, I tried to explain when and how to convince the judge that a mistrial was necessary. As I told him, "You can't unring a bell."

I also remember telling him that an effective trial lawyer pays attention to the kind of court he or she happens to be in. There are courts in urban areas where one kind of lawyerly behavior is the most effective. On the other hand, in courts located in more rural areas of our state, a good trial lawyer ensures that his behavior, and his way of speaking, take into account the nature of that kind of environment. "For example," I remember telling my young colleague, "let's say you're in a small-town courthouse. Some highly prejudicial bit of testimony has been erroneously admitted into evidence and heard by the judge. You've got to move for a mistrial. Here's an effective way to put it to the Judge:

"Your Honor, the evidence that the jury just heard is so inflammatory, so highly prejudicial, that this case simply cannot go on. Now, I know the court may feel that by just telling the jury to disregard that last statement made by the witness about my client, the case can proceed to conclusion. But, you know, Your Honor, there are some things, once you hear them, you just can't forget what you heard.

"Why, Judge, once a skunk gets in the courtroom, you can take the skunk out of the courthouse, but you can't get the smell out of the jury box.

"So, Your Honor, in fairness to my client and the system of justice which makes this country so great, you've really got to grant a mistrial."

The young lawyer listened to me attentively, nodding in appreciation at what I was telling him. Lesson learned, I remember thinking.

A few months later, my young colleague was down at the local courthouse here in Kansas City, trying one of his first cases. I went down to watch. It was a small personal injury case, and as I sat in the back of the courtroom observing the proceedings unfold, as luck would have it, some very prejudicial testimony was erroneously admitted to the jury. The young lawyer rose from his seat and requested a mistrial.

The judge was predictably reluctant to grant my associate's motion, explaining to the lawyer that he could cure the problem simply by instructing the jury to disregard the prejudicial statement. The judge and the lawyer debated the point. As I listened, I could easily see that the young lawyer was quite nervous. He spoke more rapidly than was helpful, and while he remained respectful to the judge, it was clear he was beginning to worry that he was about to lose his mistrial motion. He paused, apparently considering how best to put the point convincingly to the court. I could almost hear him thinking about what I had taught him. Then he got it. He resumed speaking. But as I said, he was nervous. He raised his arm, right finger pointing, not at the judge, but straight up at the ceiling, about to make the killer point, the one that would win the day.

"Your Honor," he intoned, now pointing directly in the direction of the jury box, "there's a skunk in the courtroom and he's ringing a bell."

GLENN E. BRADFORD
GLENN E. BRADFORD & ASSOCIATES, P.C.
KANSAS CITY, MISSOURI

There's No Questioning This Diagnosis!

T HE FOLLOWING STORY WAS TOLD TO ME WHEN I WAS A NAVAL officer in the Judge Advocate General's Corps by another Navy lawyer.

It seems the other lawyer was assigned to represent a naval recruit who had repeatedly gotten himself into trouble with the authorities. His behavior was so bad that the navy began to question his mental soundness. A psychiatric evaluation was ordered. After the results were in, the lawyer arranged to meet with his client. After all, one solution to the recruit's problem might be some kind of discharge from the service. As I heard it, the meeting went as follows:

"I received back the report from the shrink," said the lawyer.

"What's it say?" asked the recruit.

The lawyer read from the report. "It says here you're 'manipulative.'"

Not missing a beat, the recruit responded, "How can I use that?"

ANDREW L. SYMONS
INSLEE, BEST, DOEZIE & RYDER, P.S.
BELLEVUE, WASHINGTON

One Question Too Many

Ask any experienced trial lawyer and he or she will tell you. When trying a case and examining a witness, you've got to watch out for the temptation of asking a witness one question too many. It's almost always a mistake. You think you're ahead, the witness has given favorable—or at least unharmful—testimony, and you're feeling your oats. You think that with just another question or two you can really nail it down. You throw caution and good judgment to the wind. You go for it. Then you get an answer so bad that if you had a shovel, you'd start digging your own grave right there in the floor of the courtroom. In a case I tried a few years ago, it was my opponent's turn.

My partner and I represented a client who had sued a former employee. The employee had quit his job and opened a competing business unlawfully using the trade secrets he had learned while employed by our client. And what's more, when he left, he stole our client's customer list and certain computer equipment as well.

At the trial, I had just finishing examining our client's other employees. This witness had testified that the former employee had access to trade secret information and our client's customer list. However, the witness unfortunately had no direct knowledge about what the former employee did after he quit his job.

On cross-examination the former employee's attorney asked the witness whether he had ever had any personal dealings with his client. No, said the witness, he had never had any personal dealings with the former employee, but one of his salesmen had.

This is where my opponent should have thanked the witness for his testimony, smiled at the judge to show how pleased he was with his cross-examination, and sat down. Instead, he decided to plow on. His remaining cross-examination went something like this:

LAWYER: So you've never had any personal dealings with my client, but one of your salesman did, is that right?

WITNESS: That's right.

LAWYER: But you don't know what that salesman knows about my client, do you?

WITNESS: No, sir, I don't.

LAWYER: And that salesman never said anything about my client, isn't that right?

WITNESS: Well, no, sir, that's not right. He did talk about your client.

LAWYER: Well, what did he say?

(At this point in the proceedings, I was about to rise and object on the grounds of hearsay. Interestingly, the witness beat me to it.)

WITNESS: Wouldn't it be hearsay for me to testify to what I heard this salesman say about your client?

LAWYER: That's okay, you go ahead and answer the question.

WITNESS: The salesman told me that your client was a lying, cheating, back-stabbing con artist who would take advantage of anyone if given the chance.

After the laughter died down in the courtroom, my opponent and I exchanged glances. Then he shrugged and told the court, "Hmm, I guess *I* should have objected to that."

Needless to say, I was pleased with the testimony my opponent elicited.

G. TODD BURWELL
LATHAM & BURWELL, PLLC
JACKSON, MISSISSIPPI

Correspondence

Mᵧ FORMER BOSS WHEN I WAS A FEDERAL PROSECUTOR, George Beall, now one of Baltimore's finest lawyers, sent me copies of an exchange of correspondence that he says may be real, or it may not. If it isn't real, I'll bet there's something out there like it that is. In case it is real, I have changed the names and firm letterheads of the correspondents. The texts of the letters are just as I received them from George.

DEWEY, CHEATAM & HOWE
ATTORNEYS AT LAW
P.O. Box 5000
Laramie, Wyoming 62071

LAURENCE E. DEWEY
ROBIN ANN CHEATAM
N. HOWE

Telephone: (307) 555-5000
Facsimile: (307) 555-5001

_____

William Collector

Mr. A. Fancy Pants
Attorney at Law
Monroe Street
Irvine, California 92751

Dear Mr. Pants:

This firm obtained the enclosed Judgment against Defendant, Will Steele.

The Judgment remains only partially satisfied and there is due and owing as of this date principal and interest in the amount of $4,239.84. Interest accrues at the rate of $1.06 per day.

Would you please advise whether or not you would be interested in collecting on this Judgment and, if so, your fees for doing so. It's entirely possible that a letter from you to Mr. Steele will be all that's needed.

I look forward to hearing from you.

Sincerely,

DEWEY, CHEATAM & HOWE
Robin Ann Cheatam

Enclosure

A. FANCY PANTS
Attorney at Law
Monroe Street
Irvine, California 92751

Dear Ms. Cheatam:

I apologize for not getting back to you sooner, but I have been in and out of the office for the past six weeks. Seems that there's never enough time.

I want to thank you for offering me the opportunity to collect the judgment on behalf of Mr. Will Steele, but I must decline.

Without sounding pretentious, my current retainer for cases is a flat $100,000, with an additional charge of $1,000 per hour. Since I specialize in international trade and geopolitical relations between the Middle East and Europe, my clientele is very unusual and limited, and I am afraid I am unable to accept other work at this time.

I am enclosing the copy you sent of the judgment against Mr. Steele, I thank you for your thoughts. It was very nice of you.

Very sincerely,

A. Fancy Pants

Enclosure: Copy of Judgment
             For Mr. Will Steele

DEWEY, CHEATAM & HOWE
ATTORNEYS AT LAW
P.O. Box 5000
Laramie, Wyoming 62071

LAURENCE E. DEWEY   Telephone: (307) 555-5000
ROBIN ANN CHEATAM   Facsimile: (307) 555-5001
N. HOWE
————————

William Collector

Mr. A. Fancy Pants
Attorney at Law
Monroe Street
Irvine, California 92751

Dear Fancy:

I am in receipt of your letter to me regarding collection of a judgment against Will Steele.

Fancy, I've got news—you can't say you charge a $100,000 retainer fee and an additional $1,000 an hour without sounding pretentious. It just can't be done. Especially when you're writing to someone in

Laramie, Wyoming, where you're considered pretentious if you wear socks to court or drive anything fancier than a Ford Bronco. Hell, Fancy, all the lawyers in Laramie, put together, don't charge $1,000 an hour.

Anyway, we were sitting around the office discussing your letter and decided that you had a good thing going. We doubt we could get away with charging $1,000 an hour in Laramie (where people are more inclined to barter with livestock than pay in cash), but we *do* believe we could join you in California, where evidently people can get away with just about anything. Therefore, the four lawyers in our firm intend to join you in the practice of international trade and geopolitical relations between the Middle East and Europe.

Now, Fancy, you're probably thinking that we don't know anything about the Middle East and Europe, but I think you'll be pleasantly surprised to find that this is not the case. Bill Collector is actually from the Middle East—he was raised outside of Chicago, Illinois, and although those national newsmen insist on calling Illinois the Midwest, to us, if it's between New York and the Missouri River, it's the Middle East.

Additionally, although I have never personally been to Europe myself, my sister just returned from vacation there and told me lots about it, so I believe I would be of some help to you on that end of the negotiations. Larry Dewey has actually been there, although it was fifteen years ago, so you might have to update him on recent geopolitical developments. Also, Larry has applied to the Rotary Foreign Exchange Student Program for a sixteen-year-old Swedish girl and believes she will be helpful in preparing him for trips abroad.

Another thing you should know, Fancy, is that the firm has an extensive foreign language background, which I believe would be useful to you. Larry took Latin in high school, although he hasn't used it much inasmuch as he did not become a pharmacist or a priest. Norrie Howe took high school German, while Bill has mastered Spanish by ordering food at numerous local Mexican restaurants. I, myself, majored in French in college, until I realized that probably wasn't the smartest career move in the world. I've forgotten such words as *international* and *geopolitical* (which I'm not too familiar with in English), but I can still hail a taxi or find a rest room, which might come in handy.

Fancy, let us know when we should join you in California so that we can begin doing whatever it is you do. In anticipation of our move, we've all been practicing trying to say we charge $1,000 an hour with a straight face, but so far, we've haven't been able to do it. I suspect it'll be easier once we actually reach California, where I understand they charge $500,000 for one-bedroom condos and everybody (even poor people) drives a Mercedes. Anyway, because I'll be new to the area of international trade and geopolitical relations, I'm thinking of only charging $500–$600 an hour to begin with. Will that be enough to meet our overhead?

I look forward to hearing from you before you go away again for six weeks.

Sincerely,

DEWEY, CHEATAM & HOWE
Robin Ann Cheatam

P.S. Incidentally, we have advised our client of your hourly rate. She is willing to pay you $1,000 per hour to collect this judgment provided it doesn't take you more than four seconds.

GEORGE BEALL
HOGAN & HARTSON, L.L.P.
BALTIMORE, MARYLAND

Acknowledgments

My continued gratitude goes to Simon & Schuster's David Rosenthal. Our friendship has spanned twenty years, during which he has always encouraged me to write. His keen mind and uncommon conceptual talents are as responsible for this book as anything I contributed. Bill Rosen, my editor, was a pleasure to work with. His sense of what works and what doesn't, combined with his serious editorial skills, made for a very enjoyable collaboration. My wife Simma is always there, no matter what, no matter how singlemindedly self-absorbed I get. She read and assessed every story I considered, both unedited and edited. She is this book's "Everyman." And she's my everything. Lisa Phillips, my assistant, more than deserves the substantial gratitude and respect I have owed her for years. She somehow managed to keep track of all the outgoing requests for stories and the incoming responses in military precision order, much as she has done for me professionally, for years. Kim Geffert, my secretary, was also of enormous help with this project.

Many thanks once again to the National Court Reporters Association for allowing me to reprint portions of *Disorder in the Court.* The things we say when we're on the record!

And, of course, my everlasting gratitude to all the lawyers who took time from their busy professional lives to send me a favorite story.

Thank you all.

R.L.

Permissions Acknowledgments

"A Good Judge," by John W. Suthers, Executive Director, Colorado Department of Corrections, Colorado Springs, Colorado, page 114, previously appeared in *Before the Bar: A History of the El Paso County Bar Association, 1902–1995,* published in 1996.

"My Two Trips to the Supreme Court," by Martha B.G. Lufkin, Lincoln, Massachusetts, page 121: portions previously appeared in the July 1999 issue of *The Lincoln Journal.*

"A Judge's Mailbox," by the Honorable Barry G. Silverman, Judge, United States Court of Appeals for the Ninth Circuit, Phoenix, Arizona, page 127, previously appeared in *Litigation* and in *Arizona Attorney.*

"Holy Krishna," by Peter D. Baird, Lewis and Roca LLP, Phoenix, Arizona, page 208, previously appeared in *Litigation.*

"Lawyer Howe," by Gedney M. Howe III, Charleston, South Carolina, page 244, previously appeared in a privately published collection.